Reaching All Learners:

Making Differentiation Work

Bertie Kingore, Ph.D.
AUTHOR

Jeffery Kingore
DESIGN AND ILLUSTRATION

Professional Associates Publishing
www.kingore.com

Current Publications by
Bertie Kingore, Ph.D.

Alphabetters: Thinking Adventures with the Alphabet (Task cards)
Assessment: Time Saving Procedures for Busy Teachers, 4th ed.
–Assessment Interactive CD-ROM
Centers in Minutes!
–Centers CD-ROM Vol. 1: Grades K-8
–Centers CD-ROM Vol. 2: Literacy Stations, Grades K-4
Differentiation: Simplified, Realistic, and Effective
–DIfferentiation Interactive CD-ROM
Engaging Creative Thinking: Activities to Integrate Creative Problem Solving
Integrating Thinking: Strategies that Work! 2nd ed.
Growing Great Minds: Translating Research into K-4 Instruction
Just What I Need! Learning Experiences to Use on Multiple Days in Multiple Ways
Kingore Observation Inventory, 2nd ed.
Literature Celebrations: Catalysts for High-Level Book Responses, 2nd ed.
Reading Strategies for Advanced Primary Readers
Reading Strategies for Advanced Primary Readers: Professional Development Guide
Recognizing Gifted Potential: Planned Experiences with the KOI
Teaching Without Nonsense: Translating Research into Practice, 2nd ed.
We Care: A Curriculum for Preschool Through Kindergarten, 2nd ed.

FOR INFORMATION OR ORDERS CONTACT:
PROFESSIONAL ASSOCIATES PUBLISHING
PO Box 28056
Austin, Texas 78755-8056
Toll free phone/fax: 866-335-1460

Reaching All Learners
Making Differentiation Work

Grades 1 through 8

Copyright © 2007 Bertie Kingore

Published by Professional Associates Publishing

Printed in the United States of America
ISBN: 0-9787042-3-1

Table of Contents

List of Reproducible Figures

CHAPTER 4: **The Teaching Palette–**

40 Strategies for

Differentiating Instruction

INTRODUCTION

Reaching All Learners builds upon the background experiences of educators informed about differentiation and already aware of its value. This work does not propose to convince professionals of the need to differentiate but to guide educators toward more efficiently implementing the instructional differences sorely needed to ensure continuous learning for a wide-range of students.

Effective teachers clearly understand that children learn differently and enter a classroom with diverse backgrounds, varied interests, and different levels of readiness to learn specific concepts and skills. The reality is that when students represent different levels of readiness, different levels of instruction are needed. Teachers seek more information and examples that model how to differentiate lessons. They want to respond to the different needs of students and promote students' learning with less intensive preparation time.

In response to ongoing requests from administrators and teachers, this book provides specific examples and simplified procedures for differentiating instruction. Teachers and districts strive to develop their own differentiation procedures because they are the ones who know their students best. However, beginning with numerous examples to reference makes the decision-making process and customizing of instruction more efficient.

Foundational strategies for differentiating lessons include tiered instruction with product differentiation and flexible grouping. Tiered instruction is developed in Chapter 1. The management of differentiation and instruction in flexible groups is addressed in Chapter 2. Suggestions to facilitate the establishment of an effective learning environment are shared in Chapters 3. These chapters are followed by a teaching palette of forty strategies in Chapter 4 that eases the differentiation of instruction. These strategies remind teachers of interesting, effective ways to increase students' achievement and their active involvement in learning.

Kingore, B. (2007). *Reaching All Learners*. Austin, TX: Professional Associates Publishing.

PURPOSES

The intent of this book is to respond to the questions and problems that teachers confront as they implement and extend differentiation. This content supports teachers' problem solving as they:

- Implement research-based strategies to differentiate instruction.
- Base instructional decision-making upon high-yielding strategies that promote high achievement.
- Tier instructional lessons to more effectively reach all learners.
- Increase students' mental and process engagement in learning situations.
- Promote social interactions that are both content-related and learning-directed. In other words, get students talking about learning experiences.
- Access a collection of suggestions, techniques, examples, and processes that enable them to continue moving forward with differentiation while reducing frustration and excessive preparation time.

TERMINOLOGY

Differentiation is diagnosing the readiness level of each student and customizing instruction so every individual experiences continuous learning.

Tiered instruction is a differentiation strategy in which all students are taught the same essential concepts and skills at different levels of complexity in response to students' readiness and diagnosed needs.

Tiers, layers, and *levels of complexity* are used interchangeably for variety in context.

Assessment and evaluation are used as distinct terms. Assessment is the collection and analysis of information to guide instructional decisions. Evaluation is the grading or judgment of assessment information.

As such, assessment is viewed as a daily and continuous event. Evaluation occurs periodically when grades or quality decisions are needed.

FEATURES

- The text includes bulleted quick lists that enable efficient skimming to access ideas and reinforcements.
- Chart formats and checklists are used extensively to allow teachers to efficiently skim, select applications of interest, and skip unneeded information.
- A teaching palette of forty strategies for differentiating instruction is included to provide choices to select and incorporate into a differentiation plan. The analogy of a teaching palette is used to put multiple strategies at teachers' fingertips, just as a painter has a palette of colors to blend.
- Many of the strategies on the teaching palette are modeled or applied in the context of the rest of the book. Whenever a strategy is used, its icon appears in the text to remind the reader that an explanation of that strategy is developed in Chapter 4.

Kingore, B. (2007). *Reaching All Learners.* Austin, TX: Professional Associates Publishing.

CHAPTER ONE:
DIFFERENTIATING INSTRUCTION

Differentiation is teachers at work refining the art of teaching.

- It is balancing the importance of whom we teach (individuals), what we teach (content), and how we teach (process).

- It is never finished. Just as great artists are never finished perfecting artistic techniques, teachers who differentiate instruction know that differentiation will never be perfect. But they take pride in the differences they are able to make, and celebrate each instructional adjustment that enables a student to achieve.

- It is complex and demanding. Many people can deliver a lesson. Teachers, on the other hand, reach students by varying instruction to enable students to understand and extend life-long learning.

- It is how we earn the name teacher.

Educators know the importance of recognizing and responding to the different learning profiles of each student. We understand that students come to us with varied cultural and linguistic backgrounds, learning opportunities, interests, and readiness levels. We strive to identify ways for all students to succeed in learning. For some students, at some times, that translates into diverting from delivering the lesson as designated by the curriculum guide or textbook. If students function at different levels, our instruction must offer different levels of complexity. Only when lessons are differentiated are the learning needs of all individuals respected and addressed.

At its best, differentiation is not an old book with a new cover. Differentiating instruction is a strategic change in attitude and instructional objectives that is well grounded in research and the best practices of numerous educational programs.

RESEARCH BASE

Differentiated lessons are a long-standing practice in special education,

Kingore, B. (2007). *Reaching All Learners*. Austin, TX: Professional Associates Publishing.

Kingore, B. (2007). Reaching All Learners. Austin, TX: Professional Associates Publishing.

advanced placement, and international baccalaureate programs. These different programs recognize that instructional changes in content, process, and products are vital to accomplish achievement goals for the individuals in each program. To accommodate the readiness level diagnosed for each learner, differentiated lessons may involve grade-level instruction, remediation, reteaching, extension, enrichment, or acceleration. With grade-level instruction, a teacher delivers the grade-level curriculum; reteaching is a brief instructional revisit to refine a concept or skill; remediation is a longer-term instructional accommodation to rectify learning needs or develop background skills and concepts which students have not had an opportunity to learn; extensions add content depth; enrichment provides additional experiences within a topic; and acceleration elevates the pace and level of instruction and content. These instructional deliveries occur continually, in varied combinations, as teachers differentiate instruction.

Differentiated lessons evolve from a solid research base. Research documents that learning occurs when the brain seeks meaning by connecting the unknown to what is known and by chunking meaning rather than remembering lists of facts or isolated skills (Caine, Caine, Klimek, & McClintic, 2004; Sousa, 2001; Willis, 2006). The human brain has to be primed and given a target to focus on during a topic in order to construct meaningful connections to background knowledge (Wolfe, 2001). Sousa (2003) further explains the brain's role in memory by identifying the primacy-recency effect which specifies that students remember best the information they experience first in a lesson. They remember second best the information they experience last in a learning segment. An additional factor in the brain's deeper understanding is the power of emotional engagement in learning (Sousa, 2001; Sylwester, 2003; Wolfe, 2001). The brain's retention of understanding increases when there is an emotional response integrated into learning. Thus, advanced organizers, the initial few minutes of instruction, emotional engagement, and the closure experiences in a lesson are paramount to learning.

Drawing upon the work of Vygotsky (1962), teachers understand that instruction must be delivered at a difficulty level that is challenging but attainable. They endeavor to provide learning experiences in children's zone of proximal development--challenges just beyond their comfort zone that extend their learning growth. Since students' zone of proximal development varies, instruction must be provided at different levels.

Rather than rely on whole-class instruction, today's educators acknowledge that higher levels of achievement result when flexible, small groups of students work cooperatively in mixed-ability groups (Kulik, 1992; Marzano, Pickering, & Pollock, 2001; Rogers, 1998) and at other times work with the teacher at their instructional level (Gentry, 1999; National Reading Panel, 2000; National Research Council, 1999; Schumm, Moody, & Vaughn, 2000). In response to students' evolving skill levels and needs, teachers regularly schedule small-group instruction in flexible, similar-level groups. The membership of these groups changes frequently in response to the current instructional objectives.

tion to activate both mental engagement and process engagement as students' active involvement and personal processing of information increase understanding and retention.

In addition to instructional strategies that increase achievement, the teacher emerges as a key influence on students' level of achievement. Research on teacher effectiveness documents what successful adults knew from personal experiences in schools: Effective teachers create a positive effect on students' achievement and a lasting effect on students' lives. A teacher's enthusiasm for teaching and personal love of the subject matter is a model that motivates students and ultimately influences their achievement (Stronge, 2002).

Recent research clarifies the synergistic relationship of comprehension and vocabulary (ASCD, 2006; Marzano, 2004; NRP, 2000). Specifically, vocabulary is directly related to comprehension and learning achievement. Children's vocabulary level at the beginning of first grade predicts their reading ability at the end of first grade and their eleventh grade reading comprehension. Two approaches—sustained silent reading and direct instruction in subject-specific vocabulary—combine to help rescue low achievers and enhance the academic achievement of all students.

High-level thinking continues to play a vital role in learning and long-term achieve-ment for all students (Anderson & Krathwohl, 2001). Differentiate instruction to ensure that students' thinking progresses from the begin-ning levels toward more complex levels because knowledge and skills are necessary

If the highest achievement gains are an objec-tive, differentiated lessons and small group instruction are a necessity.

In regular classrooms, teachers rec-ognize student differences but may feel too stressed for time to differentiate lessons—particularly for the advanced learner (Reis et al., 2004; Westberg, Archambault, Dobyns, & Salvin, 1993). Studies show that advanced and gifted readers limited to a grade-level reading program regress on standardized tests and in their rate of progress (CAG, 1999; Reis, 2001). Whole-class instruction may continue to domi-nate despite the increased achievement gains that research substantiates when advanced-level students work for some periods of time with a teacher at their diagnosed instructional levels (Gentry, 1999; Reis et al., 2004).

Learning standards today require instruction that is based upon research regard-ing how the brain best processes information (Caine et al., 2004; Sousa, 2001; Wolfe, 2001), research in the kinds of instruction that responds to multiple modes of learning and how students learn best (Campbell & Campbell, 1999; Sternberg & Grigorenko, 1998; Willis, 2006), and research designating which instructional strategies increase achievement (Marzano et al., 2001; Shepard, 1997). For example, effective teachers weave similarities-differences and summarization into most lessons, as those are high-yield strategies documented to affect achievement. Teachers incorporate multiple learning path-ways because the more ways information is introduced to the brain the more dendritic pathways of access are created to enhance memory (Willis, 2006). Teachers plan instruc-

but not sufficient elements of understanding for long-term retention and achievement (Shepard, 1997; Wiggins and McTighe, 2005; Willis 2006).

Educators understand the research and accept today's need for differentiated instruction; however, they require translations and examples of how to activate differentiated practices. Foundational strategies for differentiating lessons include tiered instruction and product options as discussed in this chapter.

WHAT IS TIERED INSTRUCTION?

Tiered instruction is a differentiation strategy in which all students are taught the same essential concepts and skills at different levels of complexity in response to diagnosed needs. Since tiering focuses upon the same key understandings for all students, it is a particularly vital strategy responding to the current emphasis on testing and learning standards. Tiering is not making learning easier; it is providing the appropriate challenge level that enables students to thrive (Wormeli, 2006). It customizes how students' learn concepts and skills; it does not compromise what is learned.

✓ *Tiered instruction blends assessment and instruction.*

- The teacher completes a preassessment to determine what students know and then prescribes content, processes, and products at students' different readiness levels.
- The teacher organizes the students into small, flexible groups to address instruction at appropriate levels.

✓ *Tiered instruction aligns complexity to the readiness levels of students.*

- The teacher plans different kinds of instructional support and structure to expedite learning.
- The teacher provides varied levels of learning experiences within the same unit or topic to align to the readiness levels of students and respond to their best ways to learn.
- Students focus on essential concepts and skills at the different levels of open-endedness and challenge at which they are individually capable of working.

Some educators wonder if tiering is just a new name for ability grouping; however, the differences between ability grouping and tiered groups are substantial. Figure 1.1 compares the terms.

Thus, tiered groups are referred to as flexible groupings because the working arrangements and student memberships in a group vary as instructional objectives change. Flexible groups respond to student differences, match instructional objectives, and reduce the concern of labeling students if they were always in the same group. Tiered groups are a typical practice within sport teams and among artists in the fine arts fields. Now, academic applications of tiered instruction are becoming more understood and practiced.

DEVELOPING DIFFERENTIATED LESSONS

Instruction needs to be differentiated in order to enable all students to learn in mixed-ability classrooms. Tiering a lesson allows all students to learn critical concepts and skills at a level of challenge that is the most appropriate match to their individual readiness. As Wormeli (2006) asserts: *No one learns faster or better with material and tasks not geared to where they are mentally. If we're out to teach well, we'll tier* (p. 73). The steps described in Figure 1.2 delineate an effective sequence for developing differentiated lessons.

AN ELABORATION OF THE TIERED LESSON SEQUENCE

Embellishing Figure 1.2, the following discussion clarifies the process of developing

• Figure 1.1 •
Ability Groups Versus Tiered Groups

Ability Groups	Tiered Groups
The groups label student differences.	The groups respond to student differences.
The number of groups is more constant-- typically a high, middle, and low-skill group. Instruction is organized around that preset number of groups.	There is no preset number of groups. Preassessment determines how instruction is organized for a segment of learning. At times, there might be one or two groups; at other times learning readiness levels may dictate that four or more groups are needed.
Stagnate: Student membership within groups remains nearly the same for most of the year.	Flexible: Membership within groups shifts as students' needs, instructional objectives, topics, and tasks change.
Placement is based upon the assessment of past achievement.	Placement is a temporary instructional response to preassessment.
Instruction responds to students' perceived ability.	Instruction is customized to learners' readiness and profiles.
Specific concepts and skills vary with the perceived ability level of each group. Different concept and skills are taught to different groups.	The same concepts and skills are taught, practiced, or extended at varying levels of complexity to all groups.
Expectations may vary depending upon the ability level of the students.	Expectations of continuous learning for all students prevail.
Ability grouping is driven by ability labels and assessment.	Tiered grouping is driven by preassessment, ongoing assessment, and student needs.

Kingore, B. (2007). *Reaching All Learners*. Austin, TX: Professional Associates Publishing.

tiered lessons. Skim this elaboration to identify any part for which additional information would be helpful and then read further to focus on that point.

1 Skim the curriculum and learning standards to select the appropriate learning concepts and skills to target in a lesson.

Review your learning standards to identify what all students must learn. Select which essential concepts, skills, or generalizations to address, and determine which learning standards to integrate.

Determine the priorities of your lesson. Focus on what students should learn and demonstrate as a result of this experience.

2 Determine introductory-level information to share in whole class instruction.

Sharing information and introductory activities as a whole class builds a community

---

• Figure 1.2 •
Tiered Lessons

Steps

1. Skim the curriculum and the learning standards to select the appropriate learning concepts and skills to target in a lesson.
2. Determine introductory-level information to share in whole class instruction.
3. Reflect upon all available information to determine students' readiness levels, needs, and grouping options.
4. Determine which processes and products are most applicable to demonstrate learning achievement.
5. Infuse your teaching style into a curriculum activity that is appropriately challenging for most students and targets understanding of key concepts or skills.
6. Vary the task appropriately for students with fewer skills.
7. Create variations that are more complex for students ready for heightened challenge.
8. Consider instructional options to ensure that each student is mentally engaged and experiences success.
9. Determine appropriate assessment and evaluation procedures to document that each student learns the targeted concepts and skills.
10. Develop appropriate closure experiences to share through whole class instruction.

Kingore, B. (2007). *Reaching All Learners.* Austin, TX: Professional Associates Publishing.

of learners and establishes the attitude that we share a common learning purpose. Students enjoy and benefit from some work together as a class.

3 Reflect upon all available information to determine students' readiness levels, needs, and grouping options.

Preassessment is a key to differentiation.

- It provides information that enables a teacher to plan variations of the lesson so all students engage in learning at appropriate levels.
- It increases students learning success as teachers vary the lesson to connect to what students know.
- It saves instructional time by enabling the teacher to delete some aspect of the planned instruction that everyone demonstrates they know.
- It motivates students by illuminating for them what they need to know and thereby increase their interest in learning.
- It decreases the boredom that results when students continue learning experiences at the level they already know. Students are seldom bored when the learning task is a match to their readiness and interests.

Reflect upon current assessment data about students to guide decisions regarding the range of readiness that must be addressed in instruction. Valuable information is available through a combination of assessment tools, including the following.

- Preassessment results
- IEPs
- Students' profiles

- Objectives
- Students' previous work
- Conversations with students
- Observations
- Students' self-assessments
- Students' self-nominations
- Test data

If all students are at the same instructional level, whole class instruction can proceed. If a wider range is assessed, instruction must be customized and organized in small, flexible groups to maximize achievement success.

How many tiers or different learning levels are needed?

- Different quantities of levels are needed for different curricula areas and different concepts and skills in relation to learners' needs.
- Sometimes, two tiers are sufficient; at other times, three to five or more work better to match the wide range of learners.
- Teachers use a different quantity of levels to vary peer groupings. Changing the number of levels is one way to vitalize flexible groupings and ensure that students are not always in the same group.
- If multiple tiers seem overwhelming, teachers begin with two levels and complement themselves for breaking the whole-class, middle-of-the-road approach of the past.

4 Determine which processes and products are most applicable to demonstrate learning achievement.

Figure 1.3 is a checklist to guide the selection of learning processes and products. Skim the checklist when considering potential learning experiences for a lesson.

Kingore, B. (2007). *Reaching All Learners*. Austin, TX: Professional Associates Publishing.

• Figure 1.3 •

Selecting Learning Experiences

☑ Review the curriculum and teaching objectives to determine processes and products with potential for rich instructional applications that best document learning achievements.

☑ Develop a list of potential learning experiences to reach these objectives by reflecting upon suggestions in the textbook or class curriculum, reviewing any learning experiences successfully used in the past, and brainstorming additional ideas.

☑ Determine which learning experiences all students can and should do. These experiences become whole class activities. Plan whether these learning experiences should be used as an introduction activity that precedes the tiered lessons, as the focus of whole class instruction, or as a closure activity that brings everyone back together.

☑ Determine which learning experiences address specific needs of students with fewer skills and students with advanced skills. Plan to incorporate these variations in the most appropriate tiers.

☑ Analyze the potential appeal of the learning experiences. Resentment from students is likely if the tasks some students engage in are perceived as more fun or disproportionately difficult. All students benefit from a variety of processes and products that integrate multiple ways to learn.

☑ Calculate the time required to complete the learning experiences. Some experiences are short-term tasks completed in less than a single setting. Other tasks may involve several sessions or require repeated guided practice. Balance the learning time allotted across levels by:

- Varying the complexity of the learning experiences.
- Varying the quantity of the learning experiences.
- Varying the quantity of materials and resources used.
- Incorporating independent applications or research opportunities.

☑ Never lose a good idea! Refer back to your list of potential learning experiences and consider if any unused activities could be appropriately incorporated into learning stations or homework applications.

Kingore, B. (2007). *Reaching All Learners*. Austin, TX: Professional Associates Publishing.

Infuse your teaching style into a curriculum activity that is appropriately challenging for most students and targets their understanding of key concepts or skills.

From the current curriculum, select one or more grade-level learning tasks that challenge most students, is interesting, and promotes understanding of key concepts or skills. Customize that learning experience with your teaching style and preferences to accommodate students' learning profiles.

Vary the task appropriately for students with fewer skills.

Learning standards dictate skills and concepts all students must know and understand. Vary targeted grade-level skills and concepts to promote learning for students with fewer skills by incorporating the applicable instructional accommodations in Figure 1.4. Use these adaptations to prompt your decision-making about maximizing learning for students with fewer skills. Add to the list as you determine appropriate alternatives.

Create variations that are more complex for students that are ready for heightened challenge.

Vary the targeted grade-level skills and concepts for students whose skills exceed grade level by incorporating the applicable instructional accommodations in Figure 1.5. These adaptations are suggested to more efficiently lift a lesson so students with advanced skills continue their learning. Add to the list as you determine appropriate alternatives.

Consider instructional options to ensure that each student is mentally engaged and experiences success.

Plan devices to encourage students' active involvement and mental engagement, such as pair share, individual response boards, and quick sketch. Specific suggestions for mental engagement are shared in the management chapter and the teaching palette. Ensure each student participates in a variation of the learning experience that is interesting and corresponds to that student's needs and readiness.

Determine assessment and evaluation procedures to document that each student learns the targeted concepts and skills.

Plan how you will assess and evaluate to document the learning achievements of each student. Grading a test and using a rubric to grade products are frequent evaluation choices. Observation checklists and students' self-assessment are additional options.

Develop appropriate closure experiences to share through whole class instruction.

For closure, bring the class together as a community of learners to share results and discuss their processes and results. In addition to a class discussion and summarization, specific strategies such as four corners, peer-share trios, and a response round are effective closure alternatives.

Kingore, B. (2007). *Reaching All Learners.* Austin, TX: Professional Associates Publishing.

• Figure 1.4 •
Lesson Variations for Students with Fewer Skills

Rather than reduce the concept and skill level, teachers must figure out ways for struggling students to learn targeted skills and concepts. Use this list of variations for students with fewer skills as a checklist to increase the efficiency of differentiating a lesson. Skim the list to validate differentiation practices already in place, select options to implement, or prompt your brainstorming of different variations. View this chart as a developing document to use to refine and add to as often as adaptation ideas occur.

Before Direct Instruction

1. Support ELL students by providing a tape recording of the lesson content in the child's first language as an advanced organizer before the student experiences direct instruction in the targeted skills in English.

2. Provide tape recordings of fiction or nonfiction. Students listen and follow along to develop background experience before they read the text during direct instruction.

3. Discuss, model, and post a rubric of the behaviors students should demonstrate when meaningfully engaged in learning.

4. Create a support system to enable struggling students to succeed at the target level for the tasks. This system includes working with the teacher, an aide, a parent volunteer, a peer tutor, in a background group, or in a peer-share trio (similar-readiness level peers).

During Direct Instruction

5. Strive to stretch students slightly beyond their comfort zones.

6. Ensure that the instruction is interesting and engaging so that all students look forward to their learning opportunities.

7. Plan to engage students' interests through choice and content examples, such as using class experiences and students' names as positive examples incorporating skills. *On the way home yesterday, Ethan listened to three songs that were each three and one-half minutes long. What was the total time he heard music?*

8. Incorporate manipulative, three-dimensional, and printed resources so students experience learning through multiple learning modes.

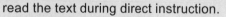
Kingore, B. (2007). *Reaching All Learners.* Austin, TX: Professional Associates Publishing.

9. Provide manipulatives, choral reading, and role-playing opportunities that students use to actively demonstrate understanding through auditory, kinesthetic, and visual modalities.

10. Plan process engagement tasks every few minutes to ensure mental engagement and assess understanding. We dare not assume that they *got it* because we *said it*. Pause to engage the students in predicting, asking and answering questions, and making personal connections using strategies, such as response rounds, topic talk, and individual response boards.

11. Incorporate pair-share. *Turn to the person next to you and discuss...*

12. Incorporate quick write opportunities to check for understanding. *For one minute, list all of the examples you can think of...*

13. Encourage children to incorporate quick sketches, symbols, and rebus writing to embellish or elaborate their responses and explanations.

14. Use more direct instruction until students begin to understand.

15. As appropriate, delegate more responsibility to students for their learning to ensure that they gain independence and management skills.

16. Provide concrete structure during the lesson. Structure the learning process so students experience a clear, linear sequence.

17. Use graphic organizers and other visual tools to structure and organize lesson content.

18. Incorporate closure techniques to aid student memory and understanding. Strategies such as riddles, summarization, and exit tickets are efficient and effective.

19. Simplify readability by using less complex versions of the content.

20. Match resources to students' background knowledge and skills. At times, these materials may need to differ from the textbook or grade-level curriculum resources. Your librarian or media specialist is a wonderful source to help secure a range of materials for every topic you teach.

Kingore, B. (2007). *Reaching All Learners.* Austin, TX: Professional Associates Publishing.

21. Engage students in echo reading in which the teacher reads one line and the group echoes or repeats the same line to model reading skills and develop comprehension. Later, students reread the passage independently.

22. Structure time more flexibly. Allow time for students to incubate content and skills.

23. Incorporate ample time for modeling and discussing examples that help students to make connections.

24. Pace the lesson sequence with planned repetition, novelty, and practice that responds to the students' rate of learning.

25. Instruct students for brief periods in small groups of two to four students when optimum achievement is required.

26. Incorporate simple rebus sentences to support phonics and the students' reading development.

27. Provide word banks.

28. Promote students' high-levels of thinking during this learning experience. All students, including those with fewer skills, benefit from opportunities to apply, analyze, synthesize, and evaluate information.

Higher levels of thinking are necessary to move students toward long-term learning rather than just short-term memorizing. Involve them in strategies such as think aloud and analyze it.

29. Support ELL students by supplementing the lesson with materials in a child's first language to augment comprehension during and after direct instruction.

30. Tape record all or part of a lesson as you work with students. As needed, students can replay a significant part to revisit or practice the skill.

31. Develop concept map relationships and webs of words as you work with students during a lesson. Students use the webs to support and structure their responses and learning tasks following the lesson.

After Direct Instruction

32. Incorporate the rebus sentences and initial sentences into direction statements so the children can read and follow directions independently.

Kingore, B. (2007). *Reaching All Learners.* Austin, TX: Professional Associates Publishing.

33. Provide blank copies of a graphic organizer to structure the content during a lesson. Students complete the organizer individually or in pairs as a follow-up to the lesson.

34. Duplicate and cut apart a completed graphic organizer used during a lesson. Students use the pieces as a manipulative to reconstruct the information.

35. Cut a summary of the content into phrases for students to use as a manipulative. Students increase comprehension by reconstructing the summary in order.

36. Use peer tutors and aides to increase individual instruction and support during study groups, guided practice of activities for targeted skills, and follow-up lessons. For example, peer teams engage in echo reading.

37. Tape-record every story read aloud to the class. Individual students can replay and follow along to practice tracking print, developing reading vocabulary, and increasing comprehension skills.

38. Have students quietly read aloud with a tape recording of text to increase fluency.

39. Use older students or parent volunteers to help develop tape recordings of fiction, nonfiction, and directions for learning experiences.

40. Use tiered centers with activities that promote practice of targeted skills and concepts. The centers should be organized with a mixed-readiness group of students for support and interaction.

Kingore, B. (2007). *Reaching All Learners.* Austin, TX: Professional Associates Publishing.

• Figure 1.5 •
Lesson Variations that Increase Challenge

To ensure all students experience continuous learning, teachers must figure out ways for advanced students to integrate targeted skills and concepts with greater depth and complexity. Consider this list of variations for students who would benefit from an increased level of challenge. The format is proposed to increase the efficiency of differentiating a lesson. Skim the list to validate current differentiation practices, select options to implement, or prompt your brainstorming of different variations. View this chart as a developing document to use to refine and add to as often as adaptation ideas occur.

Before Direct Instruction

1. Use preassessment to accurately determine students' instructional level. Promote above grade-level instruction and materials as appropriate.

2. Assess to exempt students from work they already know, understand, and are able to do.

3. Discuss, model, and post a rubric of the behaviors students should demonstrate when meaningfully engaged in learning.

During Direct Instruction

4. Strive to stretch students slightly beyond their comfort zones.

5. Communicate high expectations and personal best.

6. Ensure that instruction is targeted at advanced levels, is interesting, and is both mentally and emotionally engaging so students look forward to learning opportunities.

7. Compact and extend more than just practice the grade-level targeted concepts and skills. Analyze complexity to ensure that tasks extend beyond current mastery levels.

8. Ensure that students understand why it is important to learn the targeted concepts and skills. For example, have students interview professionals to find out how these skills are required in their work.

9. Cluster by intellectual peers and readiness level to promote the advanced language and elevated abstract and complex thinking that is typical of advanced and gifted learners.

10. Add sophistication to targeted concepts and skills by using technology and multiple texts with above grade-level readability.

11. Share with advanced learners the brain research that affects their

Kingore, B. (2007). *Reaching All Learners.* Austin, TX: Professional Associates Publishing.

learning. Advanced learners are often fascinated with how the brain works. Inform them that brain research documents they increase long-term memory by summarizing and chunking information. Practice summarization techniques to apply when pursuing topics of personal interest to develop their expertise.

12. Differentiate and elevate content rather than just offer enrichment activities that practice known concepts and skills.

13. Diversify content depth by inviting student to read and pursue individual interests and personal connections related to the topic.

14. Plan how to appropriately minimize direct instruction and increase student autonomy.

15. Assume the role of coach and facilitator more than the dispenser of knowledge. As the saying advises, become a guide on the side rather than a sage on the stage. All students need to experience feedback, encouragement, and respect from a teacher.

16. Use strategies geared to the instructional needs of advanced and gifted students, including curriculum compacting, tiering, complex content, and appropriate rate of learning.

17. To accommodate how advanced students learn best, proceed at a faster pace of instruction with minimum guided practice and repetition. Use quick sketch and think alouds to assess students' learning process during instruction.

18. Use process letters and A & E cards to efficiently assess and document understanding after instruction.

19. Provide fewer examples and require students to complete fewer examples unless continuing assessment documents that students lack appropriate understanding.

20. Elicit abstract thinking using analogies and symbols as content connections.

21. Use a Socratic Seminar approach that guides students to examine opinions or ideas logically through open-ended and probing questions that elicit students' perceptions and substantiation of their thinking.

22. Require in-text and beyond-text substantiation of ideas and generalizations with simple strategies such as before-after-support.

Kingore, B. (2007). *Reaching All Learners.* Austin, TX: Professional Associates Publishing.

23. Focus on issues and ethical connections to the topic. Use strategies such as  *analyze it* to structure responses.

24. Provide frequent opportunities for students to explore authentic text, such as researching related historical speeches instead of just reading an overview of a historical event.

25. Use biographies and autobiographies as life models of eminent people in students' fields of interest.

26. As appropriate, delegate more responsibility to students for their learning to ensure that they gain independence and management skills.

27. Involve students in searching for advanced resources and technology.

28. Create learning experiences that are more complex, require more abstract thinking, are interesting, and use advanced resources and technology.

29. Adapt the content through themes or what Erickson (2007) refers to as *conceptual lenses* to engage students' personal intellect, extend their thinking, and deepen understanding. Sample conceptual lenses include: patterns, conflict, change, power, influences, origins, and

interactions. *How is change both a cause and an effect in our world today?*

30. Immerse students in advanced levels of vocabulary and word study that incorporates academic vocabulary in specific contexts. Use affixes and roots in meaningful contexts to exponentially increase vocabulary. Use the *topic talk* and *word associations* strategies to engage vocabulary applications.

31. Initiate goal setting. Motivate students to establish personal goals and criteria for success related to their learning.

32. Use rubrics that specify abstract thinking, complexity, and depth beyond grade-level skills so students envision how to continue learning and have specific targets that challenge advance responses.

33. Demonstrate examples of superior work in order to provide concrete models of advanced products and challenge students to ever-increasing levels of excellence.

After Direct Instruction

34. Challenge students to develop high-level inferences and advanced interpretations with authentic products

Kingore, B. (2007). *Reaching All Learners.* Austin, TX: Professional Associates Publishing.

that explore significant problems and issues.

35. Require students to complete a rubric self-assessing their work before turning it in for a teacher's evaluation. Self-assessment encourages students to accept greater responsibility for their learning.

36. Provide product captions, such as the one below, that students complete to document advanced achievement and complex thinking.

37. Encourage student record-keeping. Ensure that students maintain records of their progress and personal changes as learners rather than gauge their results through comparisons with grade-level peers.

38. Organize buddies of intellectual peers to pursue advanced content in similar interests.

39. Pairs of students work together on advanced level products, such as creating summaries of a concept but omitting three to six key words or phrases. Student pairs exchange and complete the summaries to review key ideas through the perception of others.

40. Use tiered centers with activities that promote practice and extension of targeted skills and concepts. The centers should be organized with a mixed-readiness group so students have multiple opportunities to interact with all peers.

Product Caption

PRODUCT _____

This work shows that I:

I relate this to:

I elevated the depth and complexity of my response by incorporating:

❏ Essential questions	❏ Symbols or analogies	❏ Personal connections
❏ Multiple resources	❏ Complex process	❏ Advanced technology
❏ Multiple viewpoints	❏ Multiple content areas	❏ Change over time
❏ Patterns or interactions	❏ Precise academic vocabulary	

Kingore, B. (2007). *Reaching All Learners.* Austin, TX: Professional Associates Publishing.

ELEMENTS OF TIERED INSTRUCTION

Tiered instruction evolves from teachers determining how to modulate students' learning through a combination of instructional elements that relate to the readiness of the learner, allow multiple learning pathways, and influence the degree of complexity in the learning experience. Identifying these elements equips teachers with a means to more efficiently proceed with the development of tiered lessons.

When students require a variation of a lesson, reflect upon the elements of tiered instruction in Figure 1.6 to determine which could be applied to appropriately alter that lesson and promote students' continuous learning. Each element is followed by a continuum of applications that progress from simpler to more complex. (Arrows are aligned beside the applications to denote that continuum.) Develop tiered lessons by identifying the tiered elements germane to the lesson, selecting the appropriate applications on the continuum from simpler to more complex, and initiating the level of application that best fits each tier of the lesson.

• Figure 1.6 •
Tiered Elements: A Continuum of Complexity

Degree of assistance and support
- The teacher directs instruction.
- The teacher facilitates instruction.
- Students assist each other.
- Individuals are autonomous and work independently.

Degree of structure
- Familiar templates and graphic organizers are provided.
- Parameters are detailed and prescribed.
- Parameters are defined.
- Parameters are open-ended.
- Students create the organization or the structure.

Rate of instructional pacing
- Pacing is slower with extensive incubation time and multiple examples.
- Repetition and guided practice typical of the grade-level development are provided.
- Minimum repetition and practice are required.
- An accelerated rate of learning is expected; understanding is evident and quickly established.

Required background knowledge and skills
- The teacher initiates multiple beginning-level opportunities and experiences to develop background.
- Basic information and understanding is exhibited.

Kingore, B. (2007). *Reaching All Learners.* Austin, TX: Professional Associates Publishing.

- Grade-level information and understanding is evident.
- Extensive information and understanding exceeds grade-level expectations.
- Beyond grade-level expertise is required.

Concrete or more abstract

- Hands-on experiences and manipulatives are needed.
- The teacher provides open-ended graphic organizers.
- Deductive and inductive reasoning is required.
- Abstract thinking and interpretation is required.
- Metaphorical thinking and symbolism is typical.

Quantity of resources

- A single resource is provided.
- Students search to access a single resource.
- Multiple resources are provided.
- Students access multiple resources through sophisticated research and technology.

Complexity of resources

- Resources involve below grade-level readability.
- Grade-level resources are provided.
- Readability is above grade-level.
- Resources are concept dense and use complex-level vocabulary.
- The resources require sophisticated applications of technology and academic vocabulary.

Complexity of process

- A well-known and practiced process is used.
- The process is less practiced but requires few steps.
- The task is short-term and often completed in one setting.
- The task requires simple research skills.
- The task is longer-term and requires extended time on task to complete.
- The process is a new experience and requires multiple steps.
- Sophisticated research skills and independent work behaviors are required.

Complexity of product

- A single answer, fill-in-the-blank product is used.
- A typical, well-known, and frequently used product is required.
- The product integrates grade-level skills and concepts.
- The product is a new experience but the parameters are structured and clearly defined.
- The product parameters are more open-ended and unspecified.
- The product is complex and integrates advanced skills and concepts.

Complexity of the thinking skills

- Memorization or repetition is required.
- Comprehension and understanding are required.
- Application and analysis are required.
- Complex thinking requires synthesis, evaluation, and creativity.

Kingore, B. (2007). *Reaching All Learners.* Austin, TX: Professional Associates Publishing.

DIFFERENTIATING LESSONS WITH PRODUCTIVE THINKING

At times, lessons need to be differentiated for variety and appeal. I learned the importance of novelty and variety from a group of middle school students complaining about how bored they are in school. I asked them to be more specific and explain what was happening to bore them. One boy immediately responded: *I'm bored when my teacher is!* Apparently, teachers can have skills to teach and ways they teach that so obviously bore teachers even students recognize the boredom. When everyone is bored with a lesson, it benefits students and teachers to differentiate that lesson.

SCAMPER is a strategy to efficiently vary a lesson. Alex Osborn, a pioneer in productive thinking, developed a list of verbs to spur the generating of ideas. Bob Eberle (1996) rearranged those verbs as the mnemonic SCAMPER to expedite the brainstorming of new ideas and promote looking at old thoughts in new ways. When teachers become dissatisfied with the way they have taught something, they can use SCAMPER as a mental checklist to generate different ideas and multiple ways to reach diverse learners.

Use SCAMPER to:

- Add spice to a lesson.
- Incorporate high-level thinking in multiple topics and contents.
- Develop different skill applications that require students to produce instead of consume.
- Tier lessons.
- Develop independent learning tasks or learning experiences for centers.
- Uplift homework assignments.

A template for using SCAMPER to brainstorm lesson changes is included (Figure 1.7). The updated categories of Bloom's taxonomy of thinking (Anderson & Krathwohl, 2001) are added to the template to accentuate that these brainstormed lesson changes result in higher-level thinking tasks. Avoid thinking of the process as a rigid sequence. It is not required to SCAMPER in any certain order, and it is not necessary to develop ideas for all of the letters of the acronym each time. Lesson adaptations for math operations and sentence composition are provided here as examples.

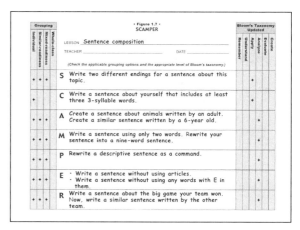

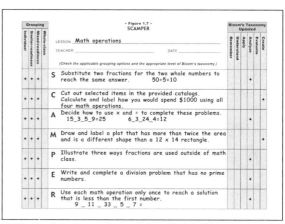

Kingore, B. (2007). *Reaching All Learners.* Austin, TX: Professional Associates Publishing.

Bloom's Taxonomy Updated								
	Create							
	Evaluate							
	Analyze							
	Apply							
	Understand							
	Remember							

• Figure 1.7 •
SCAMPER

LESSON _____

TEACHER _____   DATE _____

(Check the applicable grouping options and the appropriate level of Bloom's taxonomy.)

		S	C	A	M	P	E	R
Grouping	**Whole-class**							
	Mixed-readiness							
	Similar-readiness							
	Individual							

SCAMPER Adapted from Eberle (1996). Bloom's Taxonomy Updated by Anderson & Krathwohl (2001).

Kingore, B. (2007). *Reaching All Learners.* Austin, TX: Professional Associates Publishing.

Brainstormed lesson changes can also be tiered. Figure 1.8 repeats an activity from the math lesson and suggests how it can be simplified or varied for increased complexity.

• **Figure 1.8** •
Tiering a Math Learning Experience

LEARNING TASK: Cut out selected items in the provided catalogs. Calculate and label how you would use the items to spend $1000 using all four math operations.

Less complex

• Use at least two math operations.
• Complete the task with one other student.

More complex

• Each of the four math operations must be used twice.
• Calculate, including the sales tax on your total purchases, spending as close to $1000 as you can without exceeding that amount.
• Create a bonus point system for how close your final total is to $1000 without going over.
• With one other student, develop a rubric to evaluate the quality of your product.

DIFFERENTIATING THROUGH PRODUCT OPTIONS

Since students learn in different ways, we must provide them with options for demonstrating learning. Product options allow choice and variety in the products students complete to document their learning. As one aspect of differentiated instruction, teachers analyze products for depth and complexity, align choice with tiering objectives, and suggest or assign appropriate levels of challenge to specific students.

Product options motivate students to achieve at higher levels by:

• Incorporating a range of modalities to match students' strengths.
• Providing choice.
• Appealing to students' varied interests.
• Increasing the variety and novelty of learning responses.
• Allowing a range of complexity levels to encourage students to stretch their comfort zone and experience continuous learning.

Product options must be more than just things to keep students busy or something to do to reach closure for a topic of study. Use the checklist in Figure 1.9 to assess the quality of potential product options.

Kingore, B. (2007). *Reaching All Learners.* Austin, TX: Professional Associates Publishing.

• Figure 1.9 •
Criteria for Effective Product Options

Product options become effective learning tools when they accomplish the following.

☑ Document learning accomplishments and substantiate the acquired level of learning.

☑ Accent that students' understanding of concepts and skills is more important than the appearance and completion of the task.

☑ Require students to incorporate similarities and differences by classifying, comparing-contrasting, and creating analogies.

☑ Require summarization of key ideas rather than merely listing facts.

☑ Involve students in nonverbal as well as verbal tasks incorporating multiple modalities of their learning.

☑ Provide a tiered range of products from more simple to more complex that challenge students at different readiness levels.

☑ Encourage students to expand vocabulary pertinent to the topic or field.

☑ Promote diverse levels of thinking, depth, and complexity.

☑ Involve learning tasks that are interesting and respectful.

☑ Are enjoyable learning tasks for teachers to facilitate.

Product Option Tools

Organizing product options facilitates tiering as teachers can more readily select products and learning experiences that match learning objectives to students' interests and needs. Different formats are also useful to communicate product options to students. Tools for product options, including product lists, task cards, tic-tac-toe, and a learning options poster, are discussed to guide decisions regarding which tool or combination of tools works best.

Product Lists

An extensive list of products in Figure 1.10 provides a visual checklist for teachers to skim and facilitate the selection of appropriate products for specific teaching objectives. The intent is to more efficiently enable teachers or students to extend options beyond typical or overused products. To verify the usefulness of a product list as a differentiation tool, try this 30-second challenge.

The 30-Second Challenge
1. Think of a specific topic to teach.
2. Using only one page of the product list, skim the list for 30 seconds.
3. Try to identify two options that effectively apply to your topic.

If teachers are successful with the 30-second challenge, imagine what a range of options could be brainstormed in three minutes or how useful a product list can be to more efficiently enable teachers to match objectives and learning experiences in a lesson. Figure 1.11 guides the development of a list of product options.

Kingore, B. (2007). *Reaching All Learners.* Austin, TX: Professional Associates Publishing.

• **Figure 1.10** •

Product List

acronym	charcoal sketch	documentary	informative speech
acrostic	chart	dough art	infomercial
advertisement	children's story	dramatization	illustrations
advice column	choral reading	dramatic monologue	indexes
animation	cinquain	drawing	interview
analogy	cloze paragraph	economic forecast	invention
anecdote	coat of arms	editorial	investment portfolio
annotated bibliography	code	encyclopedia entry	invitation
announcement	collage	epilogue	jewelry
appendix	collection	epitaph	jigsaw puzzle
art gallery	comic strip	essay	jingles
audiotape	commentary	etching	job application
autobiography	comparison	evaluation	joke book
award	complaint	experiment	journal
background music	computer animation	expository writing	jump rope rhyme
ballad	computer game	fable	lab report
banner	computer program	fact file	labeled diagram
billboard	concept map (web)	fairy tale	labels
bio	constitution	fantasy	landscape design
biography	contract	family tree	large scale drawing
blueprint	conundrum	fashion article	learning center
board game	cooked concoction	fashion show script	learning profile
book	costume	festival	lecture
book jacket	couplet	fictionary	legend
book review	critique	field trip	lesson
booklet	cross section	filmstrip	letter
bookmark	crossword puzzle	flannel board	letter to the editor
bound book	cryptogram	presentation	limerick
brochure	cumulative story	flip book or chart	line drawing
bulletin board	dance	flow chart	list
bumper sticker	data sheet	folder game	lyrics
calendar	debate	folklore	mad lib
calendar quip	definition	game	magazine
calorie chart	demonstration	game show	magazine article
campaign speech	description	geometric shapes	manual
candidate platform	diagram	glossary	map w/legend
caption	dialogue	good news-bad news	maze
card game	diamante	graffiti	memoir
caricature	diary	graph	memorial
cartoon	dictionary	graphic organizer	metaphor
cereal box	diorama	greeting card	menu
certificate	directions	haiku	mobile
chamber music	director	headlines	model
character sketch	display	hidden picture	monologue
charade	document	hypothesis	montage

Kingore, B. (2007). *Reaching All Learners.* Austin, TX: Professional Associates Publishing.

mosaic
movie
movie review
movie script
mural
museum exhibit
musical composition
mystery
myth
news analysis
newsbreak
newscast
newspaper
newspaper article
nursery rhyme
obituary
observation log
ode
oil painting
opinion
oral history
outline
painting
palindrome
pamphlet
pantomime
paper chain story or
    problem
paragraph
parody
pattern
persuasive speech
photo essay
photo journal
picture
picture book
picture dictionary
picture file
play or skit
playdough
    characters/scene
poem
political cartoon
pop-up book

portfolio
post card
poster
pottery
Power Point™
    presentation
prediction
press conference
problem solution
product description
profile
propaganda sheet
protest sign
protocol
proposal
proverb
public announcement
pun
puppet /puppet show
puzzle
quiz
quiz show
questionnaire
questions
quotation
radio commentary
radio commercial
radio show
rap
reaction
readers theater
real estate notice
rebus story
rebuttal
recipe
recital
reflective essay
relief map
remedy
report, written or oral
research
response
request
requiem

requisition
resume
review
revision
rhyme
rhythmic pattern
riddles
role play
rubric
rule
sale notice
salt map
satire
satirical play
scale drawing
scavenger hunt
schedule
science fiction story
scrapbook
sculpture
self description
self-portrait
sequel
set design
short story
sign
simulation
skit
slogan
social action plan
soliloquy
song (original)
sonnet
speech
sports account
sports analysis
stencil
story
summary
survey
symbol
table
tall tale
talent show

tape recording
task card
telegram
telestitch
test
textbook
thank you note
theatre program
three-dimensional scale
time line
titles
theory
tongue twister
topographical map
transcript
travel folder
travel poster
travelogue
trial
tribute
trifold
trivia game
TV commercial
TV guide
TV program
Venn diagram
video documentary
video game
videotape
vignette
want ad
wanted poster
warning
weather forecast
weather instrument
weather report or log
web--concept mapping
website
will--legal document
wordle (word puns)
wordless book
wordplay
worksheet
yellow pages

Kingore, B. (2007). *Reaching All Learners.* Austin, TX: Professional Associates Publishing.

• Figure 1.11 •
Developing Product Options

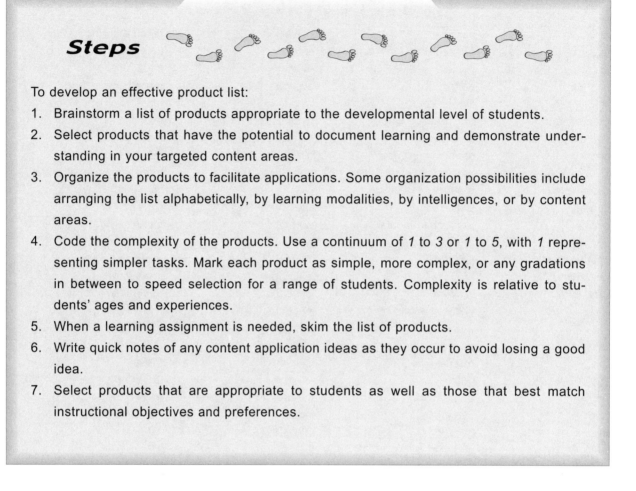

Steps

To develop an effective product list:

1. Brainstorm a list of products appropriate to the developmental level of students.

2. Select products that have the potential to document learning and demonstrate understanding in your targeted content areas.

3. Organize the products to facilitate applications. Some organization possibilities include arranging the list alphabetically, by learning modalities, by intelligences, or by content areas.

4. Code the complexity of the products. Use a continuum of *1* to *3* or *1* to *5*, with *1* representing simpler tasks. Mark each product as simple, more complex, or any gradations in between to speed selection for a range of students. Complexity is relative to students' ages and experiences.

5. When a learning assignment is needed, skim the list of products.

6. Write quick notes of any content application ideas as they occur to avoid losing a good idea.

7. Select products that are appropriate to students as well as those that best match instructional objectives and preferences.

Task Cards

Task cards describe learning experiences and products that students complete without direct teacher guidance. The card format invites a variety of applications. For any topic, teachers can prepare a set of task cards, which are then available as needed

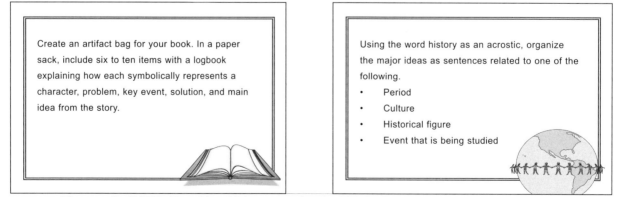

Create an artifact bag for your book. In a paper sack, include six to ten items with a logbook explaining how each symbolically represents a character, problem, key event, solution, and main idea from the story.

Using the word history as an acrostic, organize the major ideas as sentences related to one of the following.
- Period
- Culture
- Historical figure
- Event that is being studied

Kingore, B. (2007). *Reaching All Learners.* Austin, TX: Professional Associates Publishing.

throughout the segment of learning. Students select a task card as a way to demonstrate learning, or a teacher can assign specific tasks to match objectives or students' needs. Multiple cards can be displayed as product choices for students to select.

Developing the products and learning experiences for task cards can be time consuming. These suggestions make the task less daunting.

• A teacher works with two to four other teachers who teach similar content. They subdivide the topic so each teacher prepares three to five cards. When combined and duplicated, a useful set of tasks results for each classroom.

• Create generalizable task cards, such as the examples for literature and history on the previous page. The book product is designed to apply to most novels so students can read different novels at their readiness levels and still elect similar learning tasks. The history acrostic is applicable to numerous topics. Task cards extend their value as viable product options for a content area if the learning experiences and products are applicable to multiple topics and skills.

• Teachers use a simple template as the task card design, such as those in Figure 1.12. The cards are visually appealing to students yet require less time to produce when the same template is used for the set.

• Task cards should focus on tasks that require students to work at high-levels of thinking so students' efforts result in long-term learning.

Tic-Tac-Toe

Tic-tac-toe boards are a popular differentiation tool. For each topic or segment of learning, a tic-tac-toe board displays nine product options; students select and complete three in a row. Teachers initially find this an intriguing idea, but it is difficult and time consuming to create nine alternative tasks to develop a tic-tac-toe board for every topic. Consider the following solutions.

• Use examples others have created.
• Use fewer than nine options for the board.
• Use generalizable options that relate to multiple topics and applications.

When considering tic-tac-toe boards, one has to question why students have to complete three products in a row. A fifth-grade student asked: *Why do you have us do three products? Wouldn't you be pleased if I did one product really well?* If there are three specific parts to the learning that teachers want to insure students have mastered, then a tic-tac-toe may truly be the best vehicle. For example, a teacher wants students to: 1. analyze character, 2. understand the sequence of a story, and 3. determine main ideas. The teacher might then create a tic-tac-toe in which each row provides three options addressing one of those three parts, and students must select an option for each part.

Much of the time, however, completing three tasks seems an arbitrary decision based on the gimmick of a tic-tac-toe more than learning needs. Furthermore, requiring students to complete three products greatly increases the quantity of grading that teachers

Kingore, B. (2007). *Reaching All Learners.* Austin, TX: Professional Associates Publishing.

• **Figure 1.12** •
Task Card Templates

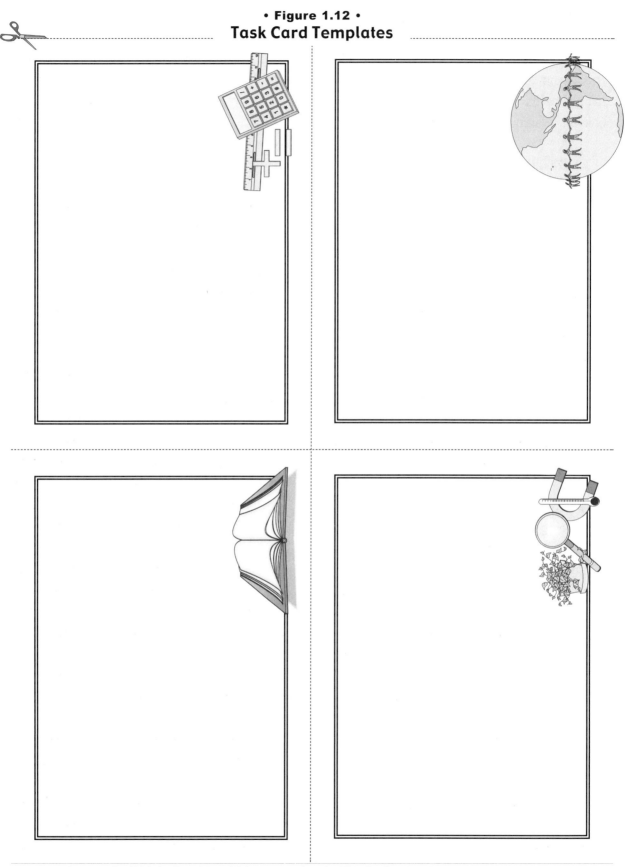

must face. Students and teachers alike are not looking for more to do.

Learning Options Poster

A learning options poster, also called a task board, is an alternative to tic-tac-toe. This option is a set of generalizable learning experiences that apply to multiple topics, concepts, and levels of student readiness. The learning experiences are enlarged as components on a poster for the classroom wall so students can easily refer to them when options are needed or assigned. Numbering each option makes it easier to refer to specific tasks. For example, a teacher might announce: *To demonstrate your understanding of this process, choose to complete either number three or five on our learning option poster.*

A teacher prepares and posts a learning options poster consisting of product choices appropriate to students and the curriculum for the entire year. At designated times, students select or teachers assign one option as the learning assignment that fits a particular segment of learning. The poster delineates product and learning task options to address the diversity of learners but avoids most of the negative elements of tic-tac-toe boards. Figure 1.13 clarifies the comparison.

With a learning options poster, no preset number of options is required. A variety of options is developed to match students' needs and reflect the number of quality learning experiences a teacher is able to incorporate. Very young or special-need learners are more successful when fewer options are presented. Two to six options are effective for these learners as

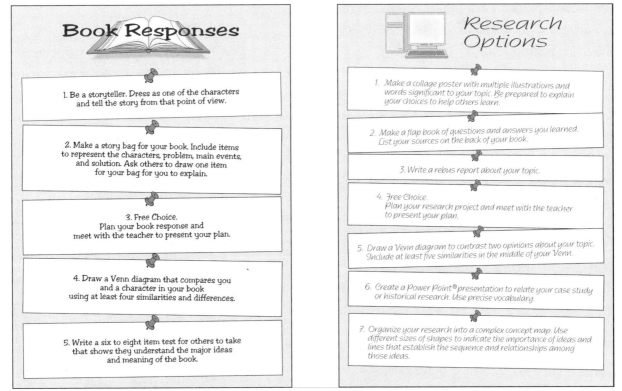

Kingore, B. (2007). *Reaching All Learners.* Austin, TX: Professional Associates Publishing.

• **Figure 1.13** •

Tic-Tac-Toe Versus a Learning Options Poster

Tic-Tac-Toe

◆ Teachers develop nine options for the current topic of study.

◆ Nine new options are developed when a different topic begins.

◆ The products can be tiered.

◆ Students must complete three tasks in a row to demonstrate learning.

◆ The board is a short-term, topic application.

Learning Options Poster

◆ Teachers develop several generalizable tasks with multiple applications.

◆ One poster presents options for applications all year.

◆ The products can be tiered.

◆ Students complete one task to demonstrate learning.

◆ The poster is a long-term curriculum application.

too many choices frustrate them and cloud their ability to reach a decision. Other students are more engaged when multiple options are provided that increase variety and novelty as they demonstrate learning.

A free-choice space is recommended as one option to encourage students to design their own product to demonstrate learning. The free-choice option should specify that students first plan their learning task and then check with the teacher before proceeding. This sequence is important as it requires students to think through their process and saves the teacher time as the student is better prepared to discuss needs and alternatives.

Teachers can develop these posters for any content area for which a set of year-long

options would be an asset. Figure 1.14 and 1.15 provide examples of learning options posters.

The learning options are customized to the developmental levels of the learners and tiered from very simple, beginning-level to quite complex, elaborated tasks. The learning options can be posted by the teacher at the beginning of the year. Or, particularly with young or special needs children, a template for the poster can be posted and the

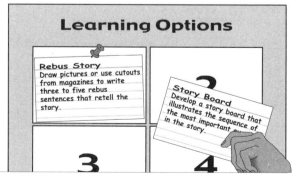

Kingore, B. (2007). *Reaching All Learners.* Austin, TX: Professional Associates Publishing.

• Figure 1.14 •
Learning Options Poster: Writing Opportunities

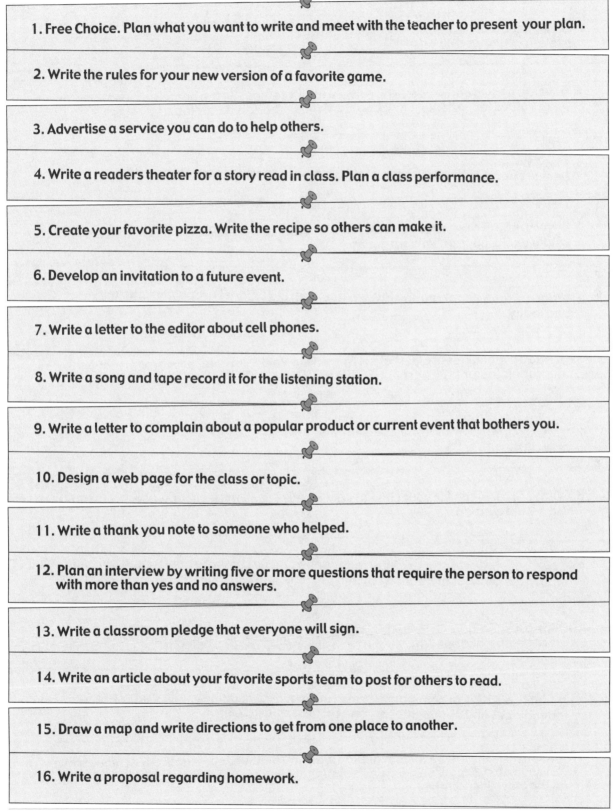

1. Free Choice. Plan what you want to write and meet with the teacher to present your plan.

2. Write the rules for your new version of a favorite game.

3. Advertise a service you can do to help others.

4. Write a readers theater for a story read in class. Plan a class performance.

5. Create your favorite pizza. Write the recipe so others can make it.

6. Develop an invitation to a future event.

7. Write a letter to the editor about cell phones.

8. Write a song and tape record it for the listening station.

9. Write a letter to complain about a popular product or current event that bothers you.

10. Design a web page for the class or topic.

11. Write a thank you note to someone who helped.

12. Plan an interview by writing five or more questions that require the person to respond with more than yes and no answers.

13. Write a classroom pledge that everyone will sign.

14. Write an article about your favorite sports team to post for others to read.

15. Draw a map and write directions to get from one place to another.

16. Write a proposal regarding homework.

Kingore, B. (2007). *Reaching All Learners.* Austin, TX: Professional Associates Publishing.

• Figure 1.15 •
Learning Options Poster: Social Studies

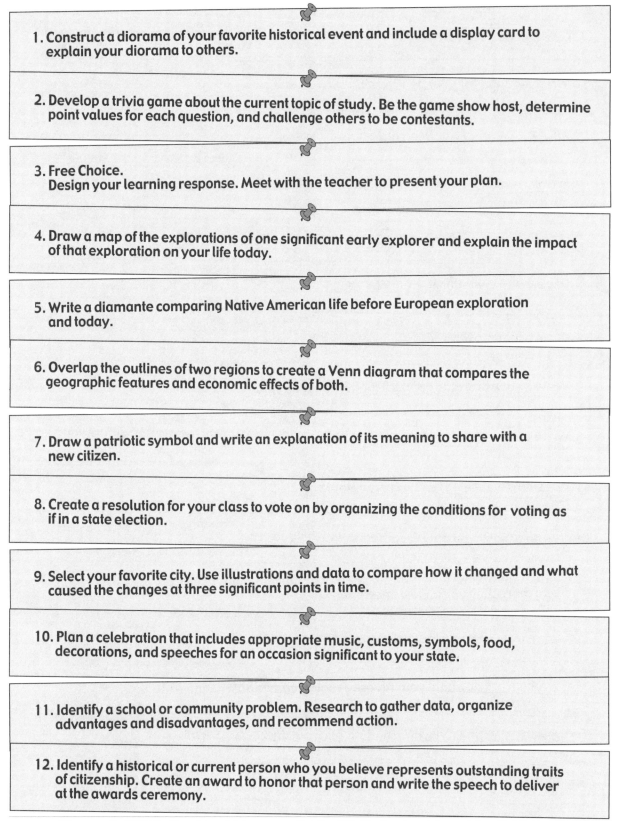

1. Construct a diorama of your favorite historical event and include a display card to explain your diorama to others.

2. Develop a trivia game about the current topic of study. Be the game show host, determine point values for each question, and challenge others to be contestants.

3. Free Choice.
   Design your learning response. Meet with the teacher to present your plan.

4. Draw a map of the explorations of one significant early explorer and explain the impact of that exploration on your life today.

5. Write a diamante comparing Native American life before European exploration and today.

6. Overlap the outlines of two regions to create a Venn diagram that compares the geographic features and economic effects of both.

7. Draw a patriotic symbol and write an explanation of its meaning to share with a new citizen.

8. Create a resolution for your class to vote on by organizing the conditions for voting as if in a state election.

9. Select your favorite city. Use illustrations and data to compare how it changed and what caused the changes at three significant points in time.

10. Plan a celebration that includes appropriate music, customs, symbols, food, decorations, and speeches for an occasion significant to your state.

11. Identify a school or community problem. Research to gather data, organize advantages and disadvantages, and recommend action.

12. Identify a historical or current person who you believe represents outstanding traits of citizenship. Create an award to honor that person and write the speech to deliver at the awards ceremony.

Kingore, B. (2007). *Reaching All Learners.* Austin, TX: Professional Associates Publishing.

tasks added over time as the class learns to independently complete a product.

In differentiated classrooms, learning options posters save instructional time. The teacher promotes independence by including options with which the class has previous experience or by designating different students as task experts for each option. Students can proceed independently or seek assistance from the designated task expert without additional teacher instruction.

* Small groups of students use the poster to plan the outcome of their group work.
* Students use the options to determine their preferred replacement tasks when preassessment validates that they have mastered a segment of learning and would benefit from different learning opportunities rather than repeating the mastered content.
* Students pursuing independent research projects refer to the poster and select products to organize their project, document their learning, and share their information with others.

Characteristics of Generalizable Product Options

In addition to the criteria for effective products in the checklist on Figure 1.9, generalizable learning products:

* Apply to multiple topics and levels.
* Are worth doing multiple times in different applications.
* Save instruction time.
* Increase students' and teachers' comfort level for different responses and different ways of learning.

* Encourage students' independence and organization skills.
* Increase success for all learners.

Teachers communicate quality to students by demonstrating both less effective and higher-level products as they discuss product options or teach students how to complete quality work. Students need to understand that quality work is the target for everyone regardless of which product they complete to demonstrate their learning. As a class, work together to generate a set of criteria that promote high quality learning responses when students are pursuing different tasks or completing open-ended tasks in different ways. Criteria, such as complexity level, depth of information, and precise vocabulary, communicate that content and understanding are more important than appearance or flash value. These criteria become the main ideas of the evaluation of the learning task. Develop rubrics that incorporate these criteria and specify levels of proficiency for each criterion. Examples of rubrics using these criteria to evaluate quality products are shared in Chapter 2.

GUIDELINES AND THINK ALOUDS

The following guidelines summarize several key ideas related to differentiating instruction. The think aloud strategy is used here to model teachers' thinking processes as they analyze differentiation issues related to these guidelines. The intent is to enable others to understand how some teachers grapple with an application and then understand it or arrive at a decision.

Kingore, B. (2007). *Reaching All Learners.* Austin, TX: Professional Associates Publishing.

Prioritize the learning objective.

Determine the objective, and then, make it the priority that guides each decision. Avoid allowing the objective to be sidetracked by less effective activities.

> *My objective is for students to compose a summary. After modeling and discussing story structure, students fold and cut four flip strips, label the strips in order with the title, beginning, middle, and end, and then write two sentences significant to each segment. The writing must be accomplished first and then children can return to each section to illustrate it with concrete or symbolic visuals. To further encourage their interpretation of content, I'll state a specific skill or concept for students to draw in the first flip section, such as: Illustrate the turning point of the story or draw and explain the main character's reaction to the problem.*
>
> *I need to differentiate that process for Jeremy, Gabriella, and Jarrod. As highly visual/spatial learners, they need to sketch first to build their ideas. Then, they can complete the written summary with more depth.*

Clarify the role of fun.

Avoid learning experiences that are only fun or just something for students to do. Fun is not a teaching objective; it is the result of great teaching using interesting and purposeful learning experiences matched to learners'

needs. Plan lessons to instruct and facilitate students' learning of significant concepts and skills. Let fun be the result of an important, well-designed learning experience, not the rationale for the lesson.

> *I used to seek activities that would be fun for my students. As I matured in my teaching, I came to realize that if my students have fun but do not experience continuous learning growth, I have really failed them. Now, when someone asks me why I am doing an activity, I share my learning objective with them and then elaborate how much students enjoyed the experience because I know them well and planned the learning experience to best match their needs and interests.*

Promote students' mental engagement.

Learning results when students' minds are in gear. Incorporate techniques that keep students actively participating. Seek ways that require every student to respond instead of whole-class demonstrations in which one student responds as others only listen or watch. Individual response boards are one device that allows all students to participate and actively respond.

> *I don't want students to be passive learners who only listen quietly and politely. I want them to get involved in the topic to increase their interest and long-term memory. Sometimes, I integrate a physical application such as movements, role-playing, or using*

manipulative devices. Many times I plan a brief active response such as a pair share to discuss a point with a peer, a quick write to record an idea or response, or brainwriting with two or three peers to develop several examples that support the point.

Promote students' process engagement.

Students benefit from time to metacognitively respond to content. Bringing their process or thinking to a conscious level expedites long-term memory.

I used to feel rushed to finish a lesson. Now, I know that students benefit more from time to process what they learn. I make time for closure devices that require them to analyze and synthesize. I keep reminding myself that the students' process engagement guides their memory better than just finishing the lesson or covering the content.

Incorporate students' interests.

In a respectful learning environment, students' interest are recognized and incorporated into learning opportunities as frequently as appropriate. Students are more actively engaged in learning when it is of personal relevance to them.

John is a low-achieving student in my middle school math class. I decided to try to ignite his enthusiasm for math by customizing more to his interests. I

encouraged him to develop math story problems about his passion for farming. He responded and surprised me with a more sophisticated application than typical for his work. With diagrams and equations, he depicted the walking distance required to relocate the irrigation pipes on his farm.

Interact with all students.

All students benefit from time and opportunities to interact with a teacher. Students differ in their degree of independence and skill but all learners benefit from a teacher's instruction, modeling, interaction, guidance, support, encouragement, coaching, and feedback--even gifted students whom some educators perceive as always making it on their own.

Kelly taught me quite a lot. As a gifted student, she had a reputation as a troublemaker. I believed that she acted out to get attention, so I made certain I gave my attention to her in positive ways--just as I did with all of the students. I made it a point to call on her in proportion to how frequently I called on other students, rather than ignore her because she always had her hand in the air. During cooperative learning, I initially assigned her roles that put her in the forefront, such as the discussion leader. Later, she learned that she enjoyed other roles, such as the illustrator of key points. As our respect for each other grew, I learned to enjoy her input and she learned to value the ideas of other students.

Kingore, B. (2007). *Reaching All Learners.* Austin, TX: Professional Associates Publishing.

Use simple content to introduce a new skill or process.

Employ more simple content, examples, and readability levels when introducing a new skill, process, or product. Students are more successful when they do not simultaneously struggle with content complexity as they initially learn how to complete a task or use a skill.

Some of my students are not very confident when we begin new material. So, I lower the challenge level to introduce a concept or skill and ensure that students understand what it is or how to do it. Then, I return to grade-level and beyond applications and try to think of examples that help them connect this learning to their background and interests. I must get them to **think they can** *rather than* **think they can't.**

Use appropriate novelty and humor to capture students' attention.

Humorous or facetious content can capture students' interests during an introduction. However, after initial modeling, demonstrations, and practice, proceed directly to applications using relevant content at grade level or beyond. Continuing to engage high-level thinking about trivial content is trivial.

This is the first time my students have encountered the SCAMPER strategy. I will have them *experience the process by using SCAMPER with the whole class to brainstorm ways to improve homework assignments. When they are successful, I will move them to use the technique individually or in small groups to stretch their thinking of more unique ways to develop their research projects and independent studies.*

Avoid doing for students what they should do for themselves.

Students' high-level thinking is prompted when they produce their own examples and develop learning applications for other students to complete. In addition to the guided practice experiences and skill sheets provided in teachers' editions and curricula materials, plan applications that require students to be producers rather than only consumers who fill-in and complete tasks designed by others.

When I teach a concept or skill, I try to think of ways for students to demonstrate their incorporation of that experience. I question: If they cannot use it, do they really own it? I ponder what I might have them develop or produce to show that they understand and can transfer that skill. For example, I am more confident that they understand a math concept when each student illustrates multiple ways to reach the solution or creates an original math story problem using that concept.

Kingore, B. (2007). *Reaching All Learners.* Austin, TX: Professional Associates Publishing.

FREQUENT QUESTIONS

Why are differentiated lessons necessary?

State and national standards stress that all students must master grade-level learning standards despite the fact that students are different and learn differently. Practicing teachers know that students enter learning situations at different levels of readiness. They tier lessons to enable all students to learn at an appropriate level of challenge-- not too hot, not too cold, but just right.

Is differentiation really fair? Is it fair when students are doing different things?

Teachers instruct students in different ways and involve students in different ways of demonstrating learning because they know students learn differently. This is fair, however, because ultimately, the result of instruction is the level of learning rather than how the learning is accomplished. All students doing the same thing may be the most unfair of all if it cramps some students and frustrates others. In a professional setting, if an adult does not draw well, is it fair to require that person to submit all ideas as sketches and symbols, or it is more important to invite that person to share ideas?

What about young and struggling children who cannot read and write well enough to use grade-level curriculum?

The art of teaching is finding solutions so all students learn and experience success.
- Seek learning experiences that accent

the head not the hand. Many graphic organizers, for example, engage both visual and linguistic learners while allowing children to demonstrate their learning with less writing.

- Provide tape recordings of text that children listen and follow along to develop background experience before they read the text independently.

- Have students quietly read aloud with a tape recording of text to increase fluency.

- Use teaching buddies--peers in the same class and students from other classes who can work with a child to provide learning support.

- Encourage children to incorporate quick sketches, symbols, and rebus writing to embellish or elaborate their written explanations.

- Use older students or parent volunteers to help develop tape recordings of fiction, nonfiction, and directions for learning experiences, such as task cards.

- Incorporate rebus sentences and initial sentences into direction statements so children can read and follow directions independently.

- Generate a short list of ideas to begin and then strive to add to your list over time to extend your options.

- Talk with specialists to elicit suggestions.

- Network with teachers experienced with your population to share ideas.

Kingore, B. (2007). *Reaching All Learners.* Austin, TX: Professional Associates Publishing.

How do I have time to differentiate?

Differentiation is highly effective teaching. Simply, we cannot afford the cost of ignoring the reality that students are at different readiness levels.

- Not having time to differentiate suggests that what we teach is more important than who we teach.
- Covering the material is not the same as teaching students so they know more today than they did yesterday.
- Remediation takes time, too.

Why is choice important?

Choice is one way to honor students' interests and modalities. Providing students choices can increase their ownership in the task and their motivation to excel. Daniels and Bizar (2004) assert that if we want to raise the kind of responsible students we claim to treasure, we have to invite them to make meaningful decisions and choices and then live with all of the consequence that choice also entails.

Should I be concerned that students with fewer skills might choose a learning task or product that is too difficult for them to complete?

Most teachers offering product options found that students are self-protective and generally quite able to select a task that is not too difficult for them. If it happens, however, provide support by asking students to work on the task in pairs or trios to increase their likelihood of success.

What can be done when students select a learning task or product that is too simple?

Initially, consider ignoring the situation. Even adults enjoy simpler choices at times, and may, for example, watch a television program beneath their intellectual level. If, however, students consistently select simple tasks they limit their learning growth and may be at risk for underachievement.

Intervene individually and briefly. State your expectation and limit the students' options. *Our objective is for you to continue learning. As you consider the product options for this assignment, I want you to select between _____ and _____.* Limit choices to the more complex options to stretch those students slightly beyond their comfort zones. They still have choice, but you have encouraged learning instead of underachievement. Most students respond positively to teachers' higher expectations when they believe we believe in them.

Kingore, B. (2007). *Reaching All Learners.* Austin, TX: Professional Associates Publishing.

CHAPTER TWO:
MANAGING THE LEARNING ENVIRONMENT

This chapter is a response to teachers' questions and concerns regarding classroom operations and the time and intensity of implementation. Teachers want to know:

How do I get it started, and how can I do it all?

GROUPING FOR INSTRUCTION

When observing a differentiated classroom, expect to see flexible grouping in action. At different times, the students are together in whole class instruction, in small groups with the student membership purposely varied with a wide range of readiness levels, in small groups planned for similar instructional needs, in pairs or trios pursuing common learning interests, or individually completing tasks.

Flexible grouping is the practice of short-term grouping and regrouping students in response to instructional objectives and students' needs. It contrasts with more stagnant grouping procedures in which students are placed in the same group or participate in whole-group instruction for all or most of the school year.

Effective differentiation requires a classroom organization and management system that promotes students' independence and responsibility, makes efficient use of instructional time, and limits the intensity of teacher preparation for instruction. In a differentiated classroom, multiple learning tasks occur simultaneously. Students frequently work in small groups on different learning experiences while the teacher directs instruction with one small group. Hence, differentiation necessitates that students learn how to work responsibly and productively, both in small groups and individually, while the teacher is engaged with other learners.

Kingore, B. (2007). *Reaching All Learners.* Austin, TX: Professional Associates Publishing.

Flexible grouping results from sound decisions. Teachers consider how they want students to interact, which grouping option is most applicable to each instructional objective, and how to activate mental engagement so most of the students are engaged in learning most of the time.

Establish specific purposes for small group instruction. Determine when instruction is best accomplished in similar readiness groups (typically used for direct teaching at students' instructional levels) or mixed-readiness groups (typically used for interactive learning tasks and activities).

GROUPING TARGET:
Some whole class learning experiences,
some small instructional groups,
some small mixed-readiness
interactive groups, and
some individual application opportunities
are provided for all students
on most days.

Skilled teachers analyze to determine the grouping option that best fits each learning objective, such as the example here of the grouping decisions concluded by one faculty. It is important to note that the *individual* category does not imply one on one instruction but refers instead to those times when a student is expected to complete a learning task alone.

Grouping decisions do not imply that one grouping option is better or worse than another. The greater concern is precisely

· **Figure 2.1** ·
Most Effective Grouping Options

Whole Class	**Mixed-Ability Small Groups**
· Introduction material · Directions · Modeling · Skills/concepts--when whole class is assessed to be at same skill level · Review · Group building · Read alouds · Closure	· Cooperative learning · Centers · Peer tutoring · Study buddies · Interest-based tasks
Similar-Ability Small Groups	**Individual Work**
· Centers · Skills/concepts--when students are assessed to be at different skill levels · When students learn at significantly different paces	· Test completion · Assessment/grading of achievement level · Individual projects · Skill sheets · Computer applications

Kingore, B. (2007). *Reaching All Learners.* Austin, TX: Professional Associates Publishing

when each option is the best instructional choice to provide the most effective achievement opportunities for each student. Use the template in Figure 2.1 to designate the most effective group option for the ongoing learning events in the classroom or school so the grouping represents informed decisions.

What size group best accomplishes the objective? For academic tasks and classroom management, less is often more effective. Experienced teachers acknowledge that most students are more actively involved in a group of two to four; in a larger group, some students are more likely to be off-task or let others assume the majority of the responsibility.

Establish the expectation that students will work with others at different times by declaring that expectation to the students:

• Figure 2.1 •
Most Effective Grouping Options

Whole Class	**Mixed–Ability Small Groups**
Similar–Ability Small Groups	**Individual Work**

Kingore, B. (2007). *Reaching All Learners.* Austin, TX: Professional Associates Publishing.

Everyone will work with everyone else at some time. Our groups are flexible and changing. Sometimes I decide. Sometimes you decide. Sometimes we randomly organize groups.

KINDS OF GROUPS

Instruction-Level Groups

Instruction-level groups are similar-readiness groups working at their instructional level directly with the teacher or other instructional leader. Tomlinson (2003) admonishes that *...it is critical during a unit to find a way to teach to a learner's need rather than only to an imaginary whole-class readiness* (p. 84). The purpose of instruction-level groups is to continue students learning at the most appropriate level of challenge through instruction that incorporates their best ways to learn. Initiate preassessments to determine students' readiness levels and form groups based upon similar readiness, background knowledge, and skills.

Skill Groups

A skill group is a short-term flexible group of students diagnosed with similar skill needs. Use continuing assessment during instruction to determine which students would benefit from reteaching, additional practice, or acceleration of skills exceeding grade level.

A & E Card Groups

Using assessment and evaluation exit cards, the teacher forms different levels of instructional, similar-readiness groups. The objective is to match instruction to students' most appropriate challenge level.

Sign-Up Groups

Sign-up is a strategy in which groups are organized by students self-nominating their participation in specific focus groups. Provide options, such as interest groups, sustained silent reading, and skills groups, for the students to select.

Background Group

A background group is typically a mixed-readiness group. The group sits together but individuals actually work alone. The teacher determines group membership and sets an academic purpose for each member, such as engage in silent reading.

Peer Tutor Pairs or Trios

Typically, peer tutors consist of one higher-skilled student helping one or two other students who are struggling or need assisted practice opportunities. Based upon diagnosed needs and personal compatibility, determine who should work together and structure a task for the pairs. As the A & E card process models, however, it is productive to allow students to volunteer to be peer tutors. Students who want to help others are more likely to be effective in the task.

Kingore, B. (2007). *Reaching All Learners.* Austin, TX: Professional Associates Publishing.

Student Choice Groups

Students chose with whom they want to compete a specific learning task designed by the teacher. Control the group sizes by specifying how many students may work in a group.

To promote student choice as well as honor both interpersonal and intrapersonal learners, simply state to the class as a learning task begins: *You may work by yourself or with one or two other people.* Students then begin the task individually or select other class members with whom to work.

Interest Based Groups

Interest groups are mixed-readiness groups whose members share a common enthusiasm for a topic. Involve students in interviews, interest inventories, or surveys; use that information to form interest groups or post the results so students can identify others who share their interests. The objective of interest groups is to honor students' interest by providing time for students to share information, resources, and motivate continued learning. Interests provide authentic reasons for student to read and learn.

Random Groups

Random groups are mixed-readiness groups with a learning purpose, such as problem solving, completing a project, or playing a content game. A variety of techniques, such as those described in Figure 2.2 on the next page, can be used to create random groups. Several of the techniques, such as question-answer, text strips, and topic vocabulary, incorporate content review and integrate skills as students form groups. After several successful experiences, invite students to suggest categories or other grouping techniques to increase their interest and self-motivated learning.

SCHEDULING FOR SUCCESS

Schedules are crucial to the success of differentiated instruction in effective learning environments. Multiple learning tasks and group configurations should occur simultaneously, and it is important that students understand what to expect. At different times:

- The teacher instructs the whole class,
- The teacher facilitates the whole class grouped into small groups,
- Some students are directly instructed by the teacher in a small group, and
- Some students work without direct teacher instruction in small groups or on independent tasks.

Teachers and students collaboratively establish routines, post a visible schedule, and develop students' understanding of what they are to do to maximize their learning opportunities. Teachers work with the students for several days (or even three to six weeks or longer with young children or special need students) to assimilate the daily schedule, the routines of classroom operation, and the learning behaviors expected from each. Alternatives are also planned to ensure that all students are meaningfully engaged in appropriate learning tasks when not working with the teacher.

Kingore, B. (2007). *Reaching All Learners.* Austin, TX: Professional Associates Publishing.

• Figure 2.2 •
Techniques for Forming Random Groups

Categories. Use various categories of things students know or can see, such as the dominate color of their clothing, the number of visible colors on the clothes, or the number of consonants in their first names. Simply name the category, ask students to look around for five seconds to orient, and then say *group time* as a signal for students to move and form groups. (Avoid categories that may be sensitive to some students or inadvertently separate students by ethnicity, such as hair color.)

Colored dots. Provide colored, peel-off dots. The number of colors you provide determines the number of groups.

1. Students randomly select a dot and then form a group with others who selected the same color.
2. If students plan their selection according to which color a friend chose, vary the technique. After students select colors, announce that each group today will be made up of one of each color.

Number off. The intended quantity of groups determines the range of numbers used. For example, for five groups, students number off one to five and then form a group with others of the same number.

Pictures. Small pictures offer multiple grouping opportunities. Laminate the pictures if you intend to use the same set all year.

1. Initial sounds. Children group with others whose pictures show something beginning with the same phoneme.
2. Categories. Children group with those whose pictures show something that fits their category, such as kinds of insects or people from a certain historical time.
3. Number. Groups form based upon how many items are pictured.

Question–answer. Provide cut strips of paper containing either a question or an answer. Students select a paper and then find the match to their question or answer. Single-answer questions result in grouped pairs of students. Questions with multiple answers result in larger groups.

Text strips. Provide lines of text cut from printed material that is familiar to students, such as nursery rhymes, songs, poems, historical documents, or speeches. Mix up the text strips. Each student selects a strip and walks around quietly reciting the words to locate others with lines to the same piece. The group is formed when all the text is complete.

Topic vocabulary. Select topic-related words to duplicate and cut apart as single words, such as six words identifying the key terms of the topic being studied. Students randomly select one of the words and form a group with others having the same word. The first task is for each group to reach a consensus of why their word is a key term. Randomly call upon one member of each group to share the term and explain the consensus.

Wrapped candy. As with colored dots, students randomly select a piece of candy and then form a group with others who selected the same kind or color of candy. For a sweet ending, invite students to talk quietly and eat the candy after they finish the group task.

Kingore, B. (2007). *Reaching All Learners.* Austin, TX: Professional Associates Publishing.

Routines

One of the attributes research reveals about effective teachers is that they carefully establish classroom routines to enable themselves and their students to work productively and efficiently (Stronge, 2002). Routines involve the development of procedures that establish responses to daily learning arrangements.

Routines and rules of operation free teachers to teach while knowing that the class can work productively. Initially, work with students to establish routines and locations for materials and equipment. Together, when appropriate, label everything with words and symbols so young and special needs children have prior experience and graphic support to successfully read the labels and manage materials well. Making these decisions together increases students' ownership in the classroom and their sense of responsibility to ensure that everything is in its correct place.

Routines allow teachers and students to be organized yet flexible. Once established, routines permit teachers to instruct small groups or conference with individuals, assured that the rest of the class can and will proceed productively with their learning responsibilities.

A comfortable and predictable class climate is one that invites participation and cooperation. Establish routines for the daily tasks, such as students working away from their tables or desks, taking attendance, handling materials, managing transitions, and working independently or in small groups productively, so that quality work and organization become a habit. Predictability frees students to relax and focus their energy on learning. Once established, the routines do not have to be rigid. Occasional change is refreshing.

Materials

Since students complete work at different times, allow students to be responsible for getting their own materials as needed. This routine makes better use of class time, avoids teachers doing it all, and prevents students from having to wait as a few helpers pass things out. This procedure is also a welcomed movement for bodily-kinesthetic learners.

Students need to be familiar with any materials and equipment they use independently. To ensure on-task behaviors, they may need time to explore and try out some materials, equipment, or manipulatives before beginning the learning tasks.

Model and teach clean-up procedures as a class routine. Students come to understand that clean-up and the reorganization of materials is a learning responsibility required anytime they use shared materials or equipment. This routine has life value as organization is an asset in most working situations.

Transitions

Transition routines are a key part of interactive classrooms. Students frequently move from one learning location to another and shift from one group configuration to

Kingore, B. (2007). *Reaching All Learners.* Austin, TX: Professional Associates Publishing.

another. To promote efficiency and productivity, teachers and students preplan transition routines, role play foot traffic patterns, and arrange classroom furniture so movement is efficient rather than disruptive.

Teachers know that classroom transitions are potential learning opportunities. Design transitions as significant learning moments by asking students to pair-share and summarize one thing they are learning before moving to the next task. Teachers can also address a quick question to students during transitions: *When I call your name, answer with a number that is greater than fifteen but less than twenty-one.* Roll call learning is a strategy on the teaching palette with further applications for transition learning moments.

Transition times need to be brief so students form the habit of responding quickly. Initially, use a stop watch to time activities requiring movement, such as switching from small groups to whole class. Then, use this measurement as the class benchmark. Before conducting that movement again, inform students how much time it usually takes and challenge them to cut one or more seconds off of the time. Keep the attitude light-hearted so students think it is a fun challenge to try to relocate quickly.

Role play and practice moving into different group configurations until students can do so in thirty to forty-five seconds. A stop watch or timer is a fun-oriented but concrete challenge for students to strive to beat the clock. Establishing this routine reduces wasted class time all year.

Learning Behaviors

Productivity is seldom an accident. Effective teachers clarify the appropriate learning behaviors expected from individuals and small groups. Rubrics are posted to designate the behaviors of productive learners and challenge students to high achievement. Additionally, teachers model and role play cooperative group techniques and appropriate behaviors for interactive small groups. Teachers use the three **R**s as a memory device for students.

- **R**esponsibility. Everyone is responsible for a duty that the rest of the group depends upon, such as being the discussion learner, materials collector, illustrator, and summarizer.
- **R**espect. Everyone shows respect to others in the group through eye contact, pleasant nonverbal responses, active listening, and sharing rather than dominating the group time and materials.
- **R**esponse. Everyone encourages positive feedback among group members and helps as needed while expecting independence from each other.

Schedule Chart

A schedule chart (also referred to as a planning chart or work board by different teachers) is a graphic to organize daily classroom activities and help students proceed more independently. It is large enough for easy viewing and includes the names of the students in flexible groups written on cards so the groups change frequently in response to instructional objectives. It incorporates cards

Kingore, B. (2007). *Reaching All Learners.* Austin, TX: Professional Associates Publishing.

with icons or words that clearly represent the routine tasks--a system that allows flexibility in changing the order of the tasks and the size and composition of the groups.

In the example in Figure 2.3, the teacher, designated by the *T,* schedules one group to directly work with and arranges other students in meaningful learning options so all students experience learning in a variety of ways. The centers require students to apply the concepts and skills posted in each center by completing activities tiered with three to four different levels of complexity for students to select. Since four centers are designated, the students understand they can work at the centers in any order and spend different amounts of time at each, yet must complete all four by the end of the week. When at computers, individuals work different software programs or levels that respond to their readiness and skill needs.

The written work varies to include composition or practice assignments tiered to student readiness. In this classroom example, Ms. Ridge believes the learning variations are important for her students and she uses this schedule chart every day. The centers and options change in response to the students' needs and the current concepts and skills that are being studied. Another teacher, less comfortable with flexible groups, might use a schedule chart similar to this for one day a week.

Grouping Chart

Some teachers use an alternative device to communicate daily organizations for learning groups. Post room arrangements or seating arrangements for different learning configurations to quickly communicate grouping decisions to students. In the middle school chart pictured here (Figure 2.4), Mr. Winkler moves a clothespin to designate the arrangement required for that day. As students enter the room, they check which seating arrangement is needed and quickly move the furniture and needed materials into place for that grouping.

The individual choice icon signals that students choose where they sit. This arrangement is useful

• **Figure 2.3** •

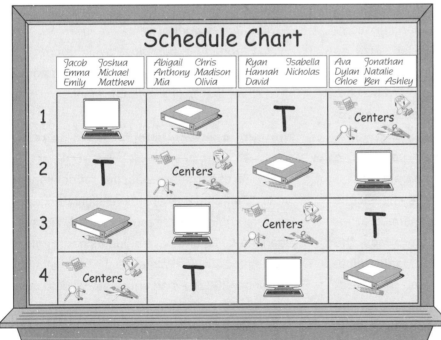

Kingore, B. (2007). *Reaching All Learners.* Austin, TX: Professional Associates Publishing.

• **Figure 2.4** •

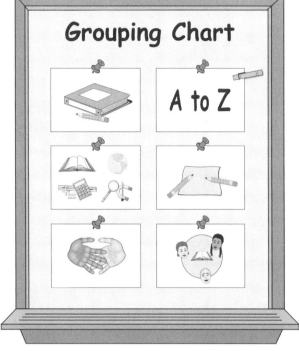

Grouping Chart

A to Z

The text club alternative enables small groups of similar-readiness level students to read different complexity levels of text to access information related to the current topic of study. Text clubs can also be mixed-readiness groups when the groups are reading the grade-level text or curriculum materials.

WHAT DO STUDENTS DO?

To promote learning, teachers work with small groups of students at their instructional pace and level. Instructional level groups are appropriate for the learning needs of students but pose the problem of what the remaining students who are not involved in the teacher's direct instruction do to continue their learning. Schedule and grouping charts provide an overview of the solution. Authentic and meaningful learning tasks, an accountability system, and *Now What* alternatives elaborate specific responses.

The ultimate goal of small group work is for the learning experiences away from the teacher to become as powerful and effective as instruction with the teacher.

Authentic and meaningful learning tasks

when the teacher instructs the whole class. In addition, as students work to complete practice applications, the teacher can call small groups for a direct skill instruction. The A to Z order signals students to sit alphabetically by last names. This order simplifies management when students hand in completed work in alphabetical order, such as during tests. The skills grouping icon is used when students work in small groups the teacher has formed for skill practice, extension, or review. These groups change regularly in response to diagnosed needs. The peer-edit or review icon sets up pairs of students working together to edit compositions or review content. Sometimes, the teacher assigns these pairs, but at other times, the pairs form randomly through student choice. The cooperative groups are used for mixed-ability tasks and are typically formed by the teacher to ensure the desired range of abilities.

Research on teacher effectiveness notes that students are more highly engaged in learning when teachers clearly identify learning goals and have students participate in authentic activities related to the topic of study (Stronge, 2002). As an anticipatory set to motivate active participation, vocalize to students how the lesson relates to them personally,

Kingore, B. (2007). *Reaching All Learners.* Austin, TX: Professional Associates Publishing.

relates to their interests, and relates to their future.

- *You are learning about pollution and ecology to avoid making the mistakes people made in the past.*
- *You are learning these math skills so no one makes a mistake that causes you to lose money, such as receiving the wrong amount of change when you purchase something.*

Authentic tasks create a student-centered personal motivation to learn (Willis, 2006). It is more authentic for students to *use* writing rather than only *do* writing to learn to write. Connect communication to the daily operation of the classroom by employing a wide array of authentic reasons to write and establishing the attitude that writing is a natural response.

> *Writing is communication.*
> *We write everyday to communicate*
> *what we do to learn and*
> *what we learned.*

Focus on authentic writing. Figure out ways to connect learning to students' lives and emphasize authentic applications of the skills students need to learn. There are a myriad of genuine, ongoing reasons for students to write in classroom that foster literacy. For a class example, brainstorm together and post an alphabetical list of everyday reasons to write so students view written communication as natural and necessary.

✓ *Implement daily goal cards.*

Goal setting is a beneficial component in the development of student responsibility. Students outline their planned accomplishments for the day on index-sized sticky-notes to post on their desks. Beside each goal, they write the estimated time it takes to accomplish that task. For closure and self-reflection at the end of the day, students use a rubric of learning behaviors to grade their productivity and effectiveness as learners on each goal. They conclude by writing a summary statement reflecting successes and their plans for the next steps.

✓ *Use quick writes.*

Request quick-write responses from students to activate mental engagement. Students produce higher quality responses when they are asked to write short notes rather than only think about a possible response. The focus during these occasions is on the quality of the information

Everyday Reasons to Write _____

Action plan	Interview	Recommendation
Address book	Invitation	Reminder
Agenda		Report/research paper
Announcement	**J**ob application	Replacement task
Apology	Jokes	Request
Assignment	Journal	Riddle
		Rubric
Birthday wish list	**K**eepsake	Rules
Brainwriting	Kudos to family or friend	
Buddy written request		**S**cavenger hunt
Budget	**L**abel	Scrapbook
Bus news	Letter	Self-evaluation
	Letters of recommendation	Short Story
Calendar of assign-	List	Sportscast
ments or events		Suggestion
Carbon copy	**M**emo	Summary
Cards	Menu	Survey
Class portfolio	Message/message board	
Classroom pledge	Minutes of meeting	**T**hank you note
Compliment	Mistake of the Day	Time schedule
	Movie review	To do list
Daily goal card		
Diary	**N**ewspaper (class	**U**pdate
Dictation	produced)	
Directions	Notes	**V**ideo game tips
		Vocabulary
Editorial	**O**bservation	Volunteer opportunity
E-Mail	Ongoing display of work	
Exit ticket	for others to read	**W**eather report
	and enjoy	Web page
Family Tree	Opinions	Word banks
Fan mail		Word wall
Field trip response	**P**enpal	
	Plan	e**X**citing reports and
Goals for self	Poem	stories
Grocery list	Postcard	
	Preview	**Y**earbook or class book
Holiday plans	Product caption	signings
Homework		
How to...	**Q**uestions	**Z**illions of notes of
	Quick writes	encouragement or
Ideas	Quotes	appreciation
In-progress note		
Instructions	**R**ecipe	

Kingore, B. (2007). *Reaching All Learners*. Austin, TX: Professional Associates Publishing.

Kingore, B. (2007). *Reaching All Learners.* Austin, TX: Professional Associates Publishing.

students produce and not on their handwriting or spelling.

✓ Develop a class portfolio.

The class portfolio is typically a photo album in which weekly entries herald the content and experiences of the class. Students take turns serving for a week as the class historian who decides which products, photographs, and details to chronologically include that most effectively represent the events during that time. The class portfolio becomes a collective scrapbook or data base in which students gain ownership in the learning process as they celebrate and evaluate completed tasks and occasions. It enables students who have been absent to see what they missed, and it helps provide new students a sense of history as they skim prior class experiences.

✓ Use technology.

Today's students have grown up with computers and are interested in technology and the efficiency it allows. When students use computers, they follow through with using spell check and have more legible work.

✓ Integrate simulations.

Simulate life experiences when class learning cannot directly use real life situations. Simulations involve students in models of life activities, such as investing in the stock market by using paper money, producing a product on an assembly line, or living in a wagon train along the Oregon Trail. Simulations are engaging and seem all the more important because of their like-life appeal. They require active participation and incorporate all of the learning modalities to enable students to be involved in their most successful ways to learn.

✓ Integrate rather than isolate skills.

Students are often more motivated to monitor and edit the errors others make in meaningful contexts rather than their own mistakes. Teachers can plant errors on written materials and invite students to actively monitor and integrate skills. Stimulate interest in homework by providing graphic organizers and papers with errors embedded that students are to locate and correct. For example, instead of completing math problems, students' homework assignment is to correct and explain the problems the teacher completed.

Oops!
Mistake!

Accountability System

Students must realize that teachers cannot make learning happen. Instead, students need to be accountable for the behaviors they demonstrate in learning situations. Success depends upon masterful teaching in a positive learning environment with students who accept responsibility. Treat students with respect and encourage them to be responsible for their own learning and their learning behaviors. An accountability system promotes quality and productivity by actively following through on students' responsibility for learning. Select the multiple components in an accountability system to fit the classroom environment.

Kingore, B. (2007). *Reaching All Learners.* Austin, TX: Professional Associates Publishing.

✓ *Debrief group time.*

Teachers value students' opinions, perceptions, and decisions. After group times, a class discussion follows to analyze effectiveness. The teacher and students offer praise and recognition of effective behaviors and work. Prompt the discussion with leading questions: *Who saw or heard someone doing well today? Who wants to share something you did well today?*

✓ *Follow up on student record keeping.*

Signal that record keeping is an important expectation and responsibility by asking about specific records and reviewing some records. It may be sufficient, for example, to simply say: *Share with the person next to you what you wrote in your learning log today.* However, some records such as goal cards and evaluation rubrics are handed in for the teacher to skim or assess further.

✓ *Communicate learning standards with posted skills.*

Post the targeted skills for a segment of learning to heighten student awareness and communicate learning objectives, In discussions and written reflections, students are responsible for explaining how they practiced or integrated those skills in their work.

✓ *Provide authentic audiences.*

Strive to provide a variety of audiences for students' work to give students more reasons to excel. Authentic audiences make the work seem more important and reinforce the idea that what students do is valued by teachers and others in and beyond the classroom. Audiences become

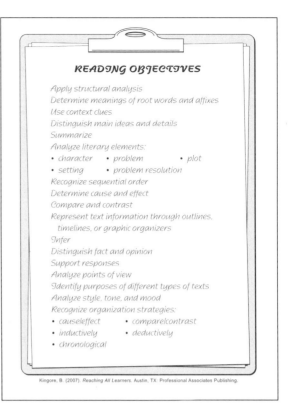

READING OBJECTIVES

Apply structural analysis
Determine meanings of root words and affixes
Use context clues
Distinguish main ideas and details
Summarize
Analyze literary elements:
• character   • problem   • plot
• setting   • problem resolution
Recognize sequential order
Determine cause and effect
Compare and contrast
Represent text information through outlines,
    timelines, or graphic organizers
Infer
Distinguish fact and opinion
Support responses
Analyze points of view
Identify purposes of different types of texts
Analyze style, tone, and mood
Recognize organization strategies:
• cause\effect   • compare\contrast
• inductively   • deductively
• chronological

Kingore, B. (2007). *Reaching All Learners.* Austin, TX: Professional Associates Publishing.

another component motivating high achievement and excellence.

Initially, students brainstorm possibilities that they then reference to determine the most relevant or preferred audience for work they are completing. Audiences within a school include displays, peers, class publications, other classes, class websites, other adults, and student-produced centers. Outside audiences include parents, grandparents, publications, other schools, district websites, museums, art galleries, school boards, centers for senior citizens, and penpals.

✓ *Develop an accountability contract.*

An accountability contract, such as Figure 2.5, specifies the behaviors that students practice to promote their responsibility for learning and to develop independent learning skills. Dialogue with the students to determine their perceptions of what students and adults alike should be accountable for in learning situations. Once established, combine those behaviors into a contract that the students and teacher sign to cement their mutual accountability for learning. Many teachers have a parent sign the contract as a means of communicating to parents the importance of a shared responsibility for learning.

✓ Use rubrics for self-evaluation.

Rubrics for student products and learning behaviors are invaluable for students' self-evaluation and to increase students' involvement and sense of ownership in evaluation procedures. As Marzano (2000) concludes, the increased application of student involvement in self-evaluation is a productive strategy resulting in personal motivation and higher achievement for many students. Guide students to self-assess and to maintain records of their own progress rather than only compare their work with peers.

Self-assessment increases students' responsibility for learning when they have a rubric as a guide to excellence before they begin a task. They are responsible for evaluating their work or learning behaviors before turning work in so the process emphasizes that what they earn relates to their degree of effort. Clearly, students who consistently evaluate their own achievement become better achievers through the process (Stiggins, 2001).

• Figure 2.5 •

Accountability Contract

❑   I am a member of a community of learners.
❑   I arrive on time.
❑   I bring my completed work.
❑   I am prepared and have materials with me.
❑   I show respect for everyone in the classroom.
❑   I care enough to do my best.
❑   I think, I try, and I participate.

STUDENT'S SIGNATURE _____   DATE _____

PARENT'S SIGNATURE _____   DATE _____

TEACHER'S SIGNATURE _____   DATE _____

Kingore, B. (2007). *Reaching All Learners.* Austin, TX: Professional Associates Publishing.

Open-ended, evaluative responses, such as Figure 2.6, are effective for students to use to critique their contributions during a group task. A rubric of learning behaviors, such as Figure 2.7, is a more specific tool that students can use daily to evaluate their goals and productive working behaviors.

Some educators evaluate students' work with a checklist that describes the desired product. A checklist, such as the Venn diagram examples in Figure 2.8 and 2.9, is useful as an inventory of the requirements of the learning task. However, even when points are added, a checklist does not explain the degrees of quality for any requirement on the list. Hence, two negative aspects result when using checklists as an evaluative tool.

Checklists increase the subjectivity of grading. I guess that's about a ___.

Checklists limit the instructional value of assessment. A checklist does not guide students' thinking about what to do to demonstrate higher achievement.

Therefore, students should use a checklist to guide their process, but have a rubric to use for evaluative thinking. The descriptors on the checklist guide students to more clearly understand the parts of the task and provide a visual reminder requiring action for closure. Ask students to physically check off each item on the checklist to avoid

• **Figure 2.6** •

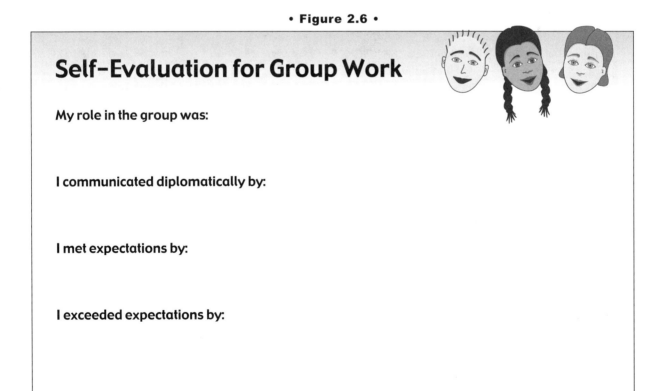

Self-Evaluation for Group Work

My role in the group was:

I communicated diplomatically by:

I met expectations by:

I exceeded expectations by:

Kingore, B. (2007). *Reaching All Learners.* Austin, TX: Professional Associates Publishing.

• Figure 2.7 •
Learning Behaviors Rubric

Below expectations	Developing learner	Practitioner	Autonomous citizen
1	**2**	**3**	**4**
Gives up easily; easily distracted	Needs some urging but works at tasks; recovers quickly when distracted	Works productively; rarely distracted; completes learning opportunities	Works conscientiously; rarely distracted; extends learning challenges
Does not follow directions	Listens; generally follows directions and rules	Cooperates; follows directions and rules	Actively listens; supports and follows directions and rules
Does not use time productively	Generally finishes task in the allotted time	Makes effective use of time	Plans; uses time efficiently
Relies on others for ideas	Beginning to use more of own ideas; needs some direction	Uses own ideas; solves problems as needed to continue learning	Self motivated; an independent thinker; creatively solves problems in learning situations
Unable to explain and apply needed skills and concepts	Needs adult support to identify and transfer skills	Transfers skills and concepts; needs little support from adults	Identifies needed skills and concepts; applies learning to new situations
Little concern for working to learn	Concerned about completing work and learning	Concerned about doing good work; understands that effort is required	Concerned for high quality; understands that effort is related to quality
Does not self-monitor	Needs support to edit and revise own work	Edits and revises own work with some assistance	Self-monitors; edits and revises own work
Summary			

Kingore, B. (2007). *Reaching All Learners.* Austin, TX: Professional Associates Publishing.

• **Figure 2.8** •

Venn Diagram–
Tier 1

Draw a Venn diagram.
Compare and contrast

_____

_____ *and*

_____

_____.

❑ Uses the Venn diagram form
❑ Labels the title and two
  categories
❑ Lists three similarities or
  differences in each section
❑ Uses accurate information
  and details
❑ Uses important words about
  the topic
❑ Writes neatly
❑ Is organized

❑ _____

❑ _____

Goes Beyond
❑ This is what I did that was
  beyond the assignment:

• **Figure 2.9** •

Venn Diagram–
Tier 2

Draw a Venn diagram.
Compare and contrast

_____

_____.

❑ Creates a diagram with two
  or more overlapping areas for
  comparisons
❑ Has a title and all of the cate-
  gories clearly labeled
❑ Lists three to six similarities
  or differences in each section
❑ Has accurate information and
  details
❑ Uses precise vocabulary and
  terminology
❑ Is legible and neatly completed
❑ Is well organized
❑ Adds visual appeal with color
  or symbols
❑ Uses three or more resources:

  _____

  _____

  _____

❑ Ends with a conclusion written
  as one or more sentences

Extends Learning
❑ Goes beyond the assignment
  by:

Kingore, B. (2007). *Reaching All Learners.* Austin, TX: Professional Associates Publishing.

the problem of students believing they are finished when they have not completed every requirement. Simultaneously, provide a rubric that students and teachers use for evaluating the quality of the work. Figure 2.10 conveys the process of combining checklists and rubrics for evaluation. Figures 2.11, 2.12, and 2.13 are rubrics at increasing levels of complexity to use when evaluating Venn diagrams at different readiness levels. Notice that each rubric classifies the requirements on the checklists into the major ideas of *appearance, thinking, information,* and *organization.*

NOW WHAT?

Now Whats are learning activities that students have previously experienced and are therefore capable of proceeding independently. As a class, brainstorm and agree upon interesting and meaningful learning tasks that students select as alternatives when they have completed all assignments with quality. Post the Now What as a list or as a learning option poster. Figure 2.14 is an example of a Now What poster in an upper elementary classroom.

Product checklists + Rubrics = Simplified, valid evaluations

• **Figure 2.10** •
Using Rubrics for Accuracy and Efficiency

Steps

1. Provide students with a copy of the checklist and the rubric before the learning task begins.

2. Discuss together both tools and how to use them to guide the process and the quality of the work.

3. Ask students to goal set by checking their target achievement level for each criterion on their copy of the rubric. Students mark their target levels with a colored pen; the date is written in the same color.

4. At the completion of the task, students self-evaluate on their copy of the rubric using a second color. They hand in the assignment and the rubric with their goal setting and evaluation clearly marked.

5. The teacher grades each assignment on the student's copy of the rubric and responds in a third color to signify that it is the final grade for recording in the grade book. Generally, the students' and teacher's evaluations match. Plan to meet briefly with any student when a discrepancy needs to be addressed.

Kingore, B. (2007). *Reaching All Learners.* Austin, TX: Professional Associates Publishing.

• **Figure 2.11** •
Venn Diagram Rubric–Tier 1

Content	I wrote.	I wrote some things.	I wrote many interesting facts and details.
POINTS:			
Detailed			
POINTS:			
Punctuation and Capitalization	do you hear the dog he is very loud	Do you hear the dog he is very loud.	Do you hear the dog? He is very loud!
POINTS:			
Cooperation			
POINTS:			
TOTAL POINTS: _____			

Adapted from: Kingore, B. (2007). *Assessment*, 4th ed. Austin, TX: Professional Associates Publishing.

• **Figure 2.12** •
Venn Diagram Rubric–Tier 2

	Appearance	Critical Thinking	Information	Organization
Getting started	Not neat *Less than 15 points*	Basic *Less than 20 points*	Little information; not accurate *Less than 20 points*	Unorganized *Less that 15 points*
On the right track	Needs more careful detail *15-16 points*	General understanding *20-23 points*	Basic facts; appropriate words *20-23 points*	Hard to follow *15-16 points*
Got it	Attractive; neat *17-18 points*	Understands content; compares and contrasts information *24-26 points*	Offers most key ideas and concepts; effective word choices; some substantiation *24-26 points*	Organized; a clear sequence *17-18 points*
Wow!	Eye catching; beyond expectations *19-20 points*	Understands concept; analyzes and evaluates content; compares and contrasts; original thinking *27-30 points*	In-depth content; precise word choices; well supported ideas *27-30 points*	Skillfully planned and sequenced; logically organized to guide others' understanding *19-20 points*

Comments

Kingore, B. (2007). *Reaching All Learners.* Austin, TX: Professional Associates Publishing.

• **Figure 2.13** •

Venn Diagram Rubric–Tier 3

	Appearance	Critical Thinking	Information	Organization
Below standard	Inadequate; not neat; little care evident *Below 15 points*	Vague; basic *Below 20 points*	Little information; not accurate *Below 20 points*	Unclear; lacks organization *Below 15 points*
Apprentice	Adequate; needs more careful work and attention to detail *15-16 points*	General under-standing; limited examination of evidence *20-23 points*	Provides basic facts and some key ideas; appropriate word choice; fair degree of accuracy *20-23 points*	Attempts to organize and sequence but is hard to follow *15-16 points*
Proficient	Attractive and visually appealing; neatly completed *17-18 points*	Understands content; compar-isons and contrasts reflect analysis of information *24-26 points*	Accurately relates major ideas and concepts; effective word choices; some appropriate substantiation *24-26 points*	Organized effectively; a clear sequence; well structured *17-18 points*
Exceeding	Eye catching; aesthetically pleasing; beyond expectations *19-20 points*	Conceptual level of understanding; comparisons reflect a thorough exami-nation of patterns, perspectives, and connections; evaluates *27-30 points*	Relates in-depth concepts and relationships; com-plex information; professional-like vocabulary; well supported *27-30 points*	Skillfully planned; logically sequenced and organized to communicate well and facilitate understanding *19-20 points*

Comments

Kingore, B. (2007). *Reaching All Learners.* Austin, TX: Professional Associates Publishing.

• Figure 2.14 •
Learning Options Poster: Now What?

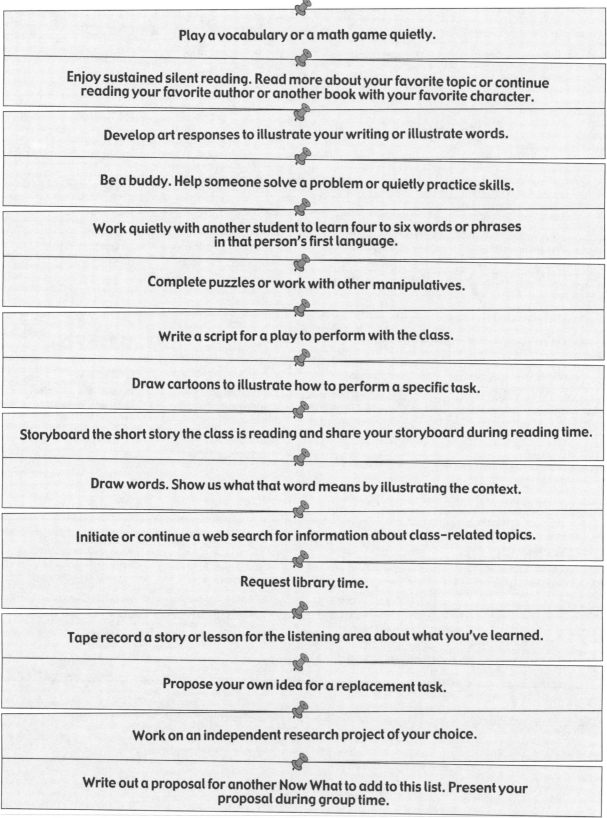

Play a vocabulary or a math game quietly.

Enjoy sustained silent reading. Read more about your favorite topic or continue reading your favorite author or another book with your favorite character.

Develop art responses to illustrate your writing or illustrate words.

Be a buddy. Help someone solve a problem or quietly practice skills.

Work quietly with another student to learn four to six words or phrases in that person's first language.

Complete puzzles or work with other manipulatives.

Write a script for a play to perform with the class.

Draw cartoons to illustrate how to perform a specific task.

Storyboard the short story the class is reading and share your storyboard during reading time.

Draw words. Show us what that word means by illustrating the context.

Initiate or continue a web search for information about class-related topics.

Request library time.

Tape record a story or lesson for the listening area about what you've learned.

Propose your own idea for a replacement task.

Work on an independent research project of your choice.

Write out a proposal for another Now What to add to this list. Present your proposal during group time.

Kingore, B. (2007). *Reaching All Learners.* Austin, TX: Professional Associates Publishing.

GETTING STARTED

If differentiation seems overwhelming because of:

- *The number of students,*
- *The wide range of readiness levels,*
- *The time constraints during the day,*
- *The emphasis on learning standards for all students,*
- *The traditional practice of whole-class instruction,*
- *The limitations of room size or materials,*
- *How things were done in the past,*
- *The demands to prepare students for the test, and*
- *The volume of content to be covered,*

then get started by seeking small steps to customize instruction.

Recognize which differentiation practices you currently use and build from there. Expand your differentiation of instruction by selecting simple starts that respond to students' learning needs while remaining comfortable within your classroom operation.

The following strategies are suggestions to consider when expanding differentiation of instruction. These realistic strategies enable practical starts toward responding to the diverse needs of individual learners.

Use strategies that are interactive and integrate multiple modalities.

Experienced teachers purposefully use learning strategies that engage students and integrate multiple modalities to honor students' best way to learn. These interactive strategies increase students' active engagement in learning as the teacher pauses periodically to elicit responses specific to the content. Figure 2.15 is a memory jogger of some of the frequently used learning strategies that interface with differentiated lessons quite effectively. Adapt any of these to enhance their usefulness.

Group within the group.

When multiple groups seems too problematic, teachers vary whole class instruction by injecting more active learning applications for students to complete in pairs during whole class instruction as the teacher moves among the students, observing, probing to clarify information, and facilitating. These applications increase students' mental engagement and provide immediate assessment information as students demonstrate their level of understanding. In addition to pair-share-square and visual tools, effective strategies on the teaching palette for grouping within the group include before-after-support, documentation chart, summarization, topic talk, and topic talk and switch. Figure 2.16 outlines a sequence for implementing this level of active engagement.

Kingore, B. (2007). *Reaching All Learners.* Austin, TX: Professional Associates Publishing.

• Figure 2.15 •
MEMORY JOGGER: FREQUENTLY USED LEARNING STRATEGIES

Strategy	Variation for Differentiation
Pair-Share or Pair-Share-Square	This technique is a cooperative learning activity that immediately gets students talking. Pose the topic or question to the whole group and say: *Talk quietly to the child next to you and decide your two best ideas.* After a couple of minutes, ask each pair to get with another pair and share their combined ideas. Use the strategy to pair ELL with a bilingual peer for language support. Occasionally, use the strategy to pair advanced students to challenge each other's more complex thinking or content depth.
Role-Play	Provide role-playing opportunities that students use to actively demonstrate understanding through auditory, kinesthetic, and visual modalities. Use the strategy to differentiate vocabulary development through students role playing key terminology in context. Differentiate the strategy to accent multiple perspectives and more complex interpretation, such as role playing a conversation between two concepts.
Interactive Questioning (Kingore, 2003)	Interactive questioning challenges students to form questions about the content to pose to other students. Differentiate the strategy by changing the focus of the questions from primarily asking others to retrieve details to queries that encourage students to question the author (get inside the author's head), to construct meaning, and support their sources (Salinger & Fleischman, 2005).
Quick Writes (Kingore, 2003)	Use the strategy to expand contexts for vocabulary by designating key terminology for students to incorporate in responses. Additionally, incorporate the strategy with summarization by asking students to write notes and sketches as information is shared; then, stop and ask students to summarize and pair-share.
Sustained Silent Reading (SSR)	SSR emerges as a significant influence on vocabulary development (ASCD, 2006). Follow SSR with opportunities for students to briefly share interesting words they found and to discuss their reading. Researchers conclude that having students discuss what they read is crucial in developing their ability to construct meaning (Cooper, 2003; Daniels & Bizar, 2005; NRP, 2000).

Kingore, B. (2007). *Reaching All Learners.* Austin, TX: Professional Associates Publishing.

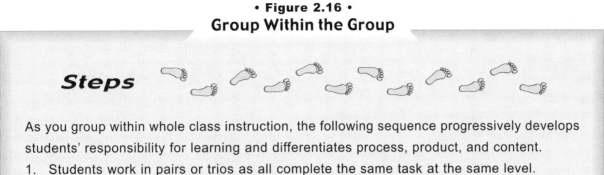

• Figure 2.16 •
Group Within the Group

Steps

As you group within whole class instruction, the following sequence progressively develops students' responsibility for learning and differentiates process, product, and content.

1. Students work in pairs or trios as all complete the same task at the same level.

   This step is a process differentiation that allows little content differentiation. It is, however, useful to increase active participation and to help students practice the behaviors for working productively in small groups.

2. Students work in pairs or trios as all complete the same task at different levels.

   This step results in product differentiation when using open-ended tasks that encourage variations in the final product. However, it promotes product and content differentiation when different levels of resources are provided for the pairs to use.

3. Students work in pairs or trios, completing different tasks at different levels.

   This step differentiates by content, process, and product. Subdivide the topic or concept and assign each pair or trio equally important parts that are at different levels of complexity.

Plan a reasonable schedule to implement instruction-level groups.

Incorporate teacher-directed, instruction level groups a few times in one content area or one class section to develop the required independent work behaviors among the students who are not working directly with the teacher. Problem solve and determine which management techniques are most effective with those learners. Then, expand to scheduling instruction group applications one day each week. Later, increase the frequency of teacher-directed instruction level groups as an ongoing learning component.

Locate direct-teaching groups to maximize students' attention.

As realtors say when selling property, the three most important considerations are location, location, location. With differentiated instruction, the same adage is true. Careful location of small groups increases the likelihood of students' successful, on-task learning behaviors.

• When direct teaching, many teachers advise arranging small group instruction at the back of the room. The teacher works with the group seated behind the other students. Students at their desks have their backs to the group working

Kingore, B. (2007). *Reaching All Learners.* Austin, TX: Professional Associates Publishing.

with the teacher. Hence, those tasks are less distracting to the students working independently. The instructional group is also more clearly focused on the teacher's instruction because it has its back to students who are working independently. The teacher can work eye-to-eye with a small group and visually oversee the rest of the class.

- Use background groups to one side at the back of the room.

Try a different assessment and grouping strategy.

Variety can be invigorating to both students and teachers. Try a different assessment strategy to determine grouping needs. The A & E card, for example, is a strategy to assess students' level of understanding of a concept or skill. The results document which level of instruction--reteach, practice, or extension--is needed to enable students to achieve so teachers can sort students into instructional groups. It also produces a pool of students who are able to, and would like to, help others learn about this content. Sign-ups is another grouping strategy for teachers to consider.

List variations that influence the complexity of a lesson.

Develop a list of the factors or techniques you find useful to help you vary the complexity of a lesson. Guide your generation of ideas by reviewing Figures 1.4 and 1.5 in Chapter 1 that include lesson variations for students with fewer skills and variations for students needing enhanced challenge. Also, consider the elements for tiering complexity on Figure 1.6 as you make your decisions.

Expand your list over time as different techniques prove effective. When you assess that a lesson needs to be tiered, challenge yourself to consider which suggestions on your list are most applicable to the specific situation. Scanning your list enables you to reach decisions more efficiently.

Use visual tools.

Visual tools are non-verbal representations of content with proven value to increase achievement (Marzano et al., 2001). They structure students' organization and formation of content and skill relationships. Since they are typically open-ended, they effectively allow students to respond at varying levels of complexity.

Several visual tools are well known and can easily be used to differentiate lessons. Experienced teachers readily adapt these tools to enhance their usefulness. A suggestion for varying each is included in the visual reminder provided in Figure 2.17

Plan a sequence to increase tiered instruction.

Tiered instruction is not an all-or-nothing concept. It is not limited to major, all-encompassing changes. Implement a small change to tier a lesson. When it works, keep it and develop an additional tiered element.

• **Figure 2.17** •

MEMORY JOGGER: FREQUENTLY USED VISUAL TOOLS

Visual Tool	Variation for Differentiation
T-Chart 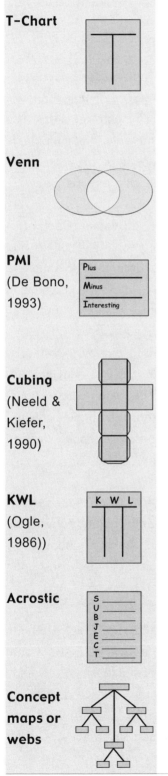	Vary the number of columns. Instead of two columns for categories and details, fold paper to create three columns, four columns, or more to organize a response and compare multiple facets of the information. Add a section across the bottom so students end with a conclusion or summary.
Venn	Vary by concluding with a summary at the bottom of the diagram. Vary by overlapping three circles to compare and contrast three different categories.
PMI (De Bono, 1993)	Vary by adding a fourth element to analyze. PMIV asks students to add a vocabulary example that is significant to the topic; PMIQ requires the addition of an essential question. Also vary by concluding with a summary statement.
Cubing (Neeld & Kiefer, 1990)	Vary by substituting different dimensions to explore. For example, label the cube with six high-level thinking skills, such as justify the results, predict the outcome, defend the conclusion, propose an alternative, create an analogy, and analyze the pattern.
KWL (Ogle, 1986))	Vary by adding a fourth element, such as KWDL for *What I will Do to learn* or KWLS for *What I Still want to know*. Ask student to conclude with a summary statement.
Acrostic	Vary by requiring students to use the acrostic term as the ending letters. Student must relate key information by organizing their ideas so the words end in the letters of the acrostic.
Concept maps or webs	Vary by challenging students to design original webs in which the graphic uses different sizes of shapes to indicate the importance of ideas, and uses lines to establish sequence and relationships.

Kingore, B. (2007). *Reaching All Learners.* Austin, TX: Professional Associates Publishing.

Over time, continue refining the process with the ongoing goal of tiering as much of instruction as necessary to enable students' to experience continuous learning.

Begin to tier instruction with an activity or lesson that you know well and have previously taught. Analyze what you can do to vary it so it is a better match to the complexity levels needed to accommodate student differences. Plan two levels that vary the complexity--not the ultimate goal in many learning situations, but a giant leap forward in getting tiered instruction started.

How long might the process of tiering instruction take? Tiered instruction is lifework. Effective teachers never stop refining their craft. The exciting reward, however, is that students' needs are more appropriately addressed with each step and their learning increases as a direct result of teachers' efforts.

Use technology as a management tool.

Use technology to save time. Technology can assist teachers as they organize data into useful forms and strive to more efficiently accomplish some of the tedious tasks associated with collecting data for differentiation. Novices to technology can seek direction and assistance from students who frequently are well-versed in technological applications or from a technology specialist in the school or district. Nancy Cook (2005) refers to technology as a savings bank for time and offers websites and practical ways to use technology when differentiating instruction. Since websites are ever changing, consider some of the following applications and network with other teachers or media specialists for website suggestions and technology resources.

Communicate with parents and students. Technology in the form of e-mail, a database, and a website enables busy teachers to efficiently maintain communication with parents and students. A class website is also useful to encourage students to communicate responses and suggestions to each other about projects and learning experiences.

Use interest surveys. Computer-based surveys can immediately collate and sort data of students' interests so teachers can incorporate those interests into lesson planning with minimum investment of time.

Access lesson planning options. Online programs, lessons, and activities are available to help teachers extend instructional ideas and access more examples of the wide-range of learning experiences needed to differentiate lessons.

Use databases. Databases streamline data management, instantly correlate information, and can identify students for placements in flexible groupings based upon assessments.

Access education updates. Updates of educational research and instructional best-practices are available online weekly through a complimentary service sponsored by the Association for Supervision and Curriculum Development. Contact ASCD for access.

Kingore, B. (2007). *Reaching All Learners*. Austin, TX: Professional Associates Publishing.

ACTIVE LEARNING TECHNIQUES BEFORE, DURING, AND AT THE END OF A LESSON

Successful teachers incorporate a potpourri of techniques to increase active learning and mental engagement. Effective techniques can require minimum preparation time yet promote high-yielding student interactions. The following discussion shares several effective interactions to review and add to your repertoire. These techniques are variations that are compatible to the best teaching practices, brain research, and cooperative learning applications.

Sousa's (2003) cognitive theory reminds us that openings and closures are vital learning opportunities for high-impact on memory. Consequently, teachers make key points first and last as they plan the structure of a lesson. Avoid beginning the day or the lesson with attendance or conducting house keeping tasks, as that may waste a prime learning opportunity. Complete these necessary duties as a break in the lesson or devise ways that students complete these tasks themselves, such as turning in an exit ticket.

Before a lesson

Be enthusiastic. Enthusiasm is contagious. A cheerful tone, upbeat voice, and quick pace set positive expectations. Show enthusiasm with body language, including an erect stance and energetic gestures.

Provide a reason for students to want to enter the classroom. A motivational teacher figures out how to jump start the day with a posted logic problem, a cartoon, a riddle, or a simple game posted for students to play as they arrive, such as tic-tac-toe or hangman.

Use purposeful devices as hooks that capture attention, pique curiosity, and establish a need-to-know attitude. The following examples work well in many classrooms.

✓ *Post initial sentences.*
Post one or more initial sentences that require students to process and apply content from previous learning experiences.

✓ *Post quotations.*
Post a quotation or daily quip that relates to the content. Students brainstorm possible connections and explain their thinking as the class begins. As an alternative, post only the first half of a quotation. Students brainstorm possible completions before the teacher shares the complete original quote and its context.

✓ *Display pictures, picture books, or a poem.*
Intriguing pictures, poems, and picture books can draw students into a topic. Even older students and adults enjoy simple, visual stimuli. Their brevity makes these choices useful and their flexible interpretations permit connections to content. They also provide great analogy and metaphor prompts to promote a teachable moment.

✓ *Share a provocative statement or question.*
Begin a lesson with a provocative statement that piques students interest. For

Kingore, B. (2007). *Reaching All Learners.* Austin, TX: Professional Associates Publishing.

example, as an introduction to a history lesson, the teacher announced: *They never saw it coming*, and proceeded enthusiastically with a litany of results before clarifying the specific historical event. A science teacher began with a discussion of stupid mistakes and segued to science connections resulting from initial errors. As an alternative, post a question to encourage active listening. *This is a key question today. Figure it out and signal when you have a significant response to share as we dissect this information.*

✓ **Create novelty situations.**

Novelty, humor, and the unexpected in lessons expedite students' attention and increase memory (Willis, 2006). Fourth grade students entered their classroom to find a pile of picture books in the way. The teacher announced: *I'm not sure what happened here but these all have to be read and organized back on this shelf. Grab a book, read it, share an idea with someone, and put that book away!* The students all read multiple books for forty minutes. They talked for several days about books they remembered from when they were young as well as books they had never seen before and puzzled over who had caused the mess. The experience prompted an authentic writing experience the next week as the class developed investigative questions they would use as they interviewed people to determine who might have dumped the books. Later, the student teacher in the first grade, with the teacher's collaboration, confessed to the deed. She explained that she saw so many new picture books

in the library, she feared the fourth graders had missed some.

In another scenario, Ms. Ellis surprised the first-grade children with a pile of empty food boxes, cans, and related grocery items. She told her class that she intended to set up a grocery store center but did not have time. The children who selected that center had to use their background experience to figure out how to organize the center as a grocery store. Extensive conversation, problem solving, and increased student ownership resulted.

Create novelty through unusual or unknown objects. An unexpected object can raise curiosity and interaction. For example, presented with a picture of a patented invention, students were challenged to figure out what function the invention might serve in the context of the social studies topic and time period of current study. *Let's figure out why this was needed in 1910.*

In another classroom, Mr. Boughman displayed a candy bar and announced: *I will place a candy bar in each group when you have figured out a plan to share it in an equitable manner.* The students' ideas led to a discussion of how fractions and math are important and useful.

Ms. Johnston uses a treasure chest to signal when an unusual object is incorporated into a lesson. The treasure chest appears in view intermittently. It can only be opened to reveal what is inside at the designated time as the lesson begins. *Today's item is _____. Why do you think this is treasured today?*

Kingore, B. (2007). *Reaching All Learners.* Austin, TX: Professional Associates Publishing.

During a Lesson

Involve students in responding or interacting approximately every fifteen to twenty minutes.

To help the brain chunk information for long-term memory, pause at an appropriate juncture of learning every fifteen to twenty minutes and guide students to process and react to the information (Sousa, 2001). In the primary grades and with some populations, elect to pause every ten minutes or as needed to ensure active engagement in learning.

Increase active participation by having students write responses before sharing their ideas in class. Signal the need for a thoughtful response by saying to them: *Take one minute and write what you think is most important before we share ideas;* or *write your best solution, and then, we will compare with each other.* Individual wipe-off boards, chalkboards, and planning sheets are effective devices for these written responses and are best used with short-answer, often single-word responses to account for differences in students' writing speeds. This sloppy-copy approach encourages more students to freely think and organize their work before they begin.

Incorporate opportunities for creative responses to content. Quick sketches, creative dramatics, role play, choral reading, readers theater, and music can be captivating and energizing. Make

a clear content connection that weaves creativity into a lesson rather that use creativity only in a tangential manner.

Provide appropriate manipulatives for students to demonstrate learning connections. For example, students have attribute blocks to position as fractions or polygons are discussed. Another time, they use a number line or time line that they mark with a large colored paper clip to hold up and show understanding. Additionally, students have response cards containing content connections, such as math symbols, high frequency words, or cause and effect that they hold up as a response. *Lollipops* (laminated circles stapled to popcycle sticks) are versions of response cards containing content connections that young students enjoy holding up to respond.

Create action responses by determining simple actions for students to demonstrate when applicable during instruction. For example, while listening to a picture book, young children wiggled their finger along their arm when the worm character was in the scene. Third grades raised their arms over their heads during their math lesson when estimates were too high. In another class, middle schoolers held up a closed hand or from one to five fingers to indicate their level of agreement to content statements or their level of understanding of a concept.

Use props to motivate interaction or communication.

Provide a novelty pointer. A magic wand or a dowel stick with a stuffed glove

Kingore, B. (2007). *Reaching All Learners.* Austin, TX: Professional Associates Publishing.

attached at one end focuses attention for tasks involving voice pointing (reading aloud as words on a chart are touched) and reading around the room (one or two students quietly read out loud the print posted in the room).

Use a timer selectively to increase the pace of student action. Asking students to think for a minute is different than the adrenaline boost promoted by stating that students have one minute and then setting the timer accordingly. The timers that visually count down seconds on an overhead or projected computer screen are effective, but a stop watch or kitchen timer also work well.

Closure

Make it a priority in your lesson structure to leave a minimum of two to five minutes for closure. Reviewing key ideas at the end of the class makes sense and provides an opportunity to use writing as a management and assessment tool. Similar to the exit tickets and 3-2-1 strategies on the teaching palette, another popular closure technique is *three stars and a wish* in which students list three things that went well and one request.

Mnemonic devices can be incorporated as a closure task. Mnemonics, or memory devices, are best remembered when individuals are actively involved in developing the device and when it synthesizes a concept rather than isolated facts. Work with students to develop a mnemonic device to remember specific content. The device might be a memorable statement students relate to their

experiences, an acronym listing letters to prompt generalizations, or an analogy expressing a specific relationship. A first grader reasoned: *Compound words are like addition and contractions are like subtraction.*

Work together to develop a summary. One of the most effective strategies for increasing achievement is summarization. It helps students strengthen their accountability for learning. Several strategies on the teaching palette invite summarizing, such as note taking, process letter, and analogies.

Create a cloze summary. Provide a well-constructed summary of the information or concept but have three to five blanks where essential information or key vocabulary terms are omitted. In pairs, students complete the cloze summary and then compare choices as a group.

Use the STOP technique. As an oral review technique when time is very short, students respond to STOP in this adaptation of Paterson's (2005) technique.

Started by: _____.
Topic is: _____.
Opportunity to learn by: _____.
Purpose for learning this is: _____.

Build a consensus of the most significant information. Students work in pairs for two minutes to develop ideas and quickly write a list of key concluding ideas. In a small

Kingore, B. (2007). *Reaching All Learners*. Austin, TX: Professional Associates Publishing.

group or whole class, pairs take turns sharing one idea on their list. Other students raise hands if that idea is also on their list. The teacher writes on the board or overhead ideas recorded by many students as a consensus of key points.

Challenge students to develop questions. Students work in pairs for two minutes to pose and write questions essential to the topic. The questions are read as a closure and then used to begin the lesson the next time with a question and answer exchange.

End with a group or class meeting. Each student briefly shares one conclusion, key idea, or interesting point about the topic or concept.

SUPPORT SYSTEMS

Plan learning experiences that stretch students just beyond their comfort zone of mastery to continue learning. The goal is for all students to work at a level that is challenging but attainable (Vygotsky, 1962; Willis, 2007). To do so, students need support for their efforts to learn and alternatives for support, feedback, and encouragement when the teacher is not available. Support systems include adults, peers, and strategies that bridge the gap between what is known and what needs to be learned for all students, including regular learners and special needs students--learning disabled, physically challenged, ELL, struggling, and accelerated learners.

People in the support system

Adults

- Identify staff members and central office coordinators who can assist with resources, training, or strategies. Resource specialists may be available to assist or peer coach in the classroom.
- Network with teachers experienced with your population to share ideas.
- Meet with media specialists or librarians to access their resources for materials in an array of levels to match students' range of reading readiness.
- Identify ESL administrators who are also resourceful in providing materials and tape recordings in students' first languages to help develop background knowledge before working extensively in English.
- Train aides and parent volunteers to support struggling students' success with target level tasks.

Peers

- Use the pair-share-square strategy as students problem solve.
- Seek students from other classes who want to work with a child to provide practice, learning support, and encouragement.
- Utilize peers and aides to increase individual instruction and support during study groups, guided practice of targeted skills, and follow-up lessons. For example, peer teams engage in echo reading.
- Complete silent reading tasks in a background group to provide peer support and follow-up responses.

Kingore, B. (2007). *Reaching All Learners*. Austin, TX: Professional Associates Publishing.

- Train students as task or skill experts-- students experienced with a specific learning task or skill--so they can answer questions and provide help as needed. Many teachers post a digital photograph of these assistants as positive recognition and to inform others of the assistant's identity. (Students with fewer skills can learn in advance how to do a task and then benefit from the opportunity to serve as the task assistant.)

- Support vocabulary building with ELL students by providing occasions when they work with a bilingual student to bridge English with the students' first language. Center and small group settings are productive occasions for students to provide language support.

- Provide opportunities for a bilingual student or student with greater English proficiency to pair-read text material with a student in the student's first language to support accessing the information in English.

- Try *2 B 4.* Mr. Ramos practices *2 B 4* in his fifth grade class--the students ask *two* other students *before* asking the teacher. This technique promotes independence from the teacher and encourages a community of students helping each other learn.

Strategies in the Support System

- Provide and model graphic organizers that help students process and organize information.

- Implement strategies that enable all learners to access and comprehend print.

- Use echo reading.

- Tape record directions when explaining information and processes to the class.

Students replay as needed.

- Provide tape recordings of text that children follow along to develop background experience and increase comprehension before they read independently.

- Teach students to quietly read aloud with a tape recording of text to increase fluency.

- Provide recordings of text material in a student's first language to support accessing the information in English.

- Highlight the topic sentences and key passages in the text to guide struggling readers to focus on a shorter amount of print to assimilate the major ideas. This highlighting is most beneficial when completed by one who understands the material and summarizes well.

- Use text clubs.

- Incorporate jigsaws with complex material.

- Use buddies for paired reading and review.

- Use computers as tools to support learners. Computer software incorporates an amazing range of levels and allows an individualized pace for learning. Computer applications have proven value in building academic vocabulary (NRP, 2000), and math skills (Willis, 2006).

- Provide copies of lecture notes for absent students. Arrange for another student to make a copy of notes and collect copies of learning materials to share when the absent student returns. This process enables peer support with a written record that guides the student working to complete missed learning opportunities.

Kingore, B. (2007). *Reaching All Learners.* Austin, TX: Professional Associates Publishing.

- Use the information from A & E cards to arrange opportunities for students to elect to be facilitators who help others learn.
- Encourage students to self-nominate targeted skill instruction by signing-up for the skills for which they need practice or clarification.
- Promote vocabulary building. A greater academic vocabulary increases comprehension and enhances cognitive processing. Hence, vocabulary needs to be developed purposefully in meaningful contexts to support and increase comprehension.
- As they read, ask students to list any more complex words they think might be important as they read. Later, the teacher or peer assistant can use those words to respond directly to that student's vocabulary needs and aid comprehension.

FREQUENT QUESTIONS

How can I do it all?

Prioritize, be selective and move forward slowly. Plan three steps or applications you are interested in implementing. Then, prioritize and set into action those three changes.

Kids get too noisy when I am not working with them. What can I do about noise levels?

There is a difference between chaos and a learning buzz. Concretely establish the desired range of volume. Role play the different levels of sound on a continuum from what is preferred to what is out of control. Noise problems tend to reoccur, so be prepared to revisit earlier discussions and role play again.

Conduct a class problem-solving meeting to elicit students' ideas. They may feel more responsible about noise control when they help to establishing the parameters.

Talk softly at times to make students listen more carefully. Deliberately lowering the volume of a voice can create attention.

How can I get my students more mentally engaged during instruction?

While you have to find your own way, some techniques that worked well for other teachers may prompt your decisions.

- Create smaller groups.
- Use individual response boards.
- Incorporate students' interests as often as it is appropriate.
- Use quick sketch responses for variety and multiple-modality processing.
- Pause more frequently to elicit an active response from students about the content.

Do I have to differentiate learning tasks? I am more comfortable assigning the same thing to everyone.

Our own past learning experiences in schools may have lead us to be used to the same learning tasks for all. Today, however, we know more about the different ways students learn and we recognize that students enter a learning segment with varied background knowledge and experiences. We provide different learning tasks to increase their learning success.

How do I respond to students who question the differences in assignments?

Learning environments of the past have conditioned students to expect the same tasks for all of the class.

*   Believe it yourself. It is most difficult to convince students what you don't believe in and what you fail to authentically incorporate as well as model.
*   Promote differences as an asset rather than a question of fairness. Try a think aloud with your class to share your reasoning.

As I observe you working, I think about how to help each of you learn. My job is to plan opportunities that provide you with the best ways to successfully increase what you understand and know how to do. I know that some of you need to talk over ideas to understand, so I provide time for you to talk about our information. Yet, some of you do better with images instead of words, so I plan times to have you complete a quick sketch or storyboard before *we proceed with learning. Since people learn in different ways, I often must think of learning experiences and assignments that differ.*

Doesn't whole class instruction save time?

Whether or not whole class instruction saves time depends upon the readiness level of the students. If all students are at the same level of readiness, learning can occur quite efficiently with whole class instruction. When students demonstrate different levels of readiness, however, whole class instruction proves less efficient. It may take less class time to complete a whole-class lesson, but if many students did not learn, reteaching must commence and will certainly require extended time.

Kingore, B. (2007). *Reaching All Learners.* Austin, TX: Professional Associates Publishing.

CHAPTER THREE:
74 TIPS FOR EFFECTIVE LEARNING ENVIRONMENTS

This potpourri of guidelines is a collection of insights and practices evolving from the effective ideas of a myriad of teachers striving to differentiate instruction. Some of the suggestions relate to one grade level more than another, but all are shared here for teachers to skim and consider while reaching management decisions or problem solving instructional concerns. The suggestions help generate solutions to classroom-operation issues and needs relevant to differentiation so the teaching energy concentrates on instruction and fostering the continuous learning of all students.

TEACHER'S ROLE

1. Take teaching and learning beyond the factual level to conceptual thinking that is critical to deeper understanding. Students with well developed conceptual structures in the brain are better able to process the massive amounts of incoming information and transfer knowledge (Erickson, 2007, p. 39).

2. Assess before beginning a segment of learning. Continually assess and evaluate students' progress and needs to guide instructional decisions, form grouping options, and determine further relevant learning experiences.

3. Make an honest effort to do something to enable continuous learning.

4. Invite parent involvement. Inform parents of the targeted concepts and skills through weekly or monthly calendars and letters. Provide suggestions about how to interact with a child when reading together to increase parents' confidence that their home nurturing mirrors the school's objectives.

Kingore, B. (2007). *Reaching All Learners.* Austin, TX: Professional Associates Publishing.

5. Accept that a teacher cannot differentiate as much when new to teaching or new to a content area. Differentiation proceeds most naturally with teachers who are familiar with their grade level curriculum and have classroom management experience.

6. Incorporate a discovery or inquiry approach to require students to grapple with problems and possibilities.

7. Coach to facilitate continual growth.

8. Accept that *fair* does not mean doing everything alike with all students. Students must access information with different paces and modalities, yet that is fair because the outcome is learning.

9. Call on all learners. All students benefit from a teacher's positive recognition and challenge.

10. Increase active learning and active listening with the whole class.
    • Integrate a system to randomly call on students.
    • Ask students to share both examples and nonexamples.
    • Invite students to embellish, paraphrase, or summarize each other's responses.

11. Make eye contact and recognize individuals. It is important to bend down to be at the same level as a young child.

12. Be an active listener. Attend and respond. Tell the student if time is not momentarily available and schedule a realistic period to meet to talk and continue the process.

13. Communicate expectations with clearly developed rubrics. Negotiate with your students and post a learning behavior rubric so all know and agree upon the appropriate behaviors expected when working independently, in groups, or at learning stations.

14. Practice wait time when questioning students to give them time to engage in higher-level thinking. Also, model wait time when responding to student behaviors. Pausing to reflect before reacting encourages a more thoughtful response and leads students to think a teacher is wiser.

15. Develop a list of products and learning activities that engage students. Continually trying to think of products is much slower than skimming a list of successful options to determine products with a best match to the learning objective. Many times, the list stimulates a different idea as teachers skim and ponder possibilities.

16. Limit the number of behavior rules for the classroom. Less is often more effective for students to remember and for the teacher to monitor. I actually established one rule that handles most student questions: *Do everything you can to help yourself and others learn.* When asked about a behavior, I usually respond: *How will that help everyone learn?*

Kingore, B. (2007). *Reaching All Learners.* Austin, TX: Professional Associates Publishing.

17. Implement mini-lessons to redirect behaviors when the learning process bogs down. Incorporate a three to five minute mini-lesson to problem solve with the class ways to resolve conflicts, such as using the schedule chart, working quietly, using materials or equipment correctly, and completing goal cards and record keeping accurately.

18. Establish off-limits times. Teachers need to conduct a direct-teaching lesson with one group without being interrupted by others. Concrete props, such as the following, can communicate when a teacher may not be disturbed.
    - Display a whimsical *Do Not Disturb* sign similar to ones that are used in hotels.
    - Post a picture of a desert island. Use a stand-up picture frame to hold a picture of a deserted island with the sand shape made from sand paper.
    - Wear a tiara. *One does not interrupt royalty without permission.*
    - Put on a hat or headband that is only worn during these times.

ACCOUNTABILITY, QUALITY, AND ACHIEVEMENT

19. Avoid doing for students what students should be doing for themselves.

20. Establish expectations with the class. Students who feel ownership in establishing classroom expectations are more likely to be responsible learners.

Guide students in a discussion of work behavior parameters and clarify which behaviors are nonnegotiable. Developing positive work behaviors with students avoids many of the potential behavior problems.

21. Work with students to develop criteria and practice scoring both strong and weak product responses to clarify criteria and develop their understanding of evaluative reasoning.

22. Facilitate students' analysis of incorrect answers on learning tasks and tests to identify the flawed reasoning.

23. Allow students to create questions as often as answer questions. Challenge them to pose prompts that require more complex thought and communication than typical of questions with *yes* or *no* answers.

24. Focus on the researched high-yield strategies affecting students' achievement, particularly similarities-differences, summarization, note taking, and reinforcing-recognizing effort. Endeavor to implement those strategies within most lessons.

25. Lead students to understand that success and higher achievement result from persistence and effort rather than luck or easy tasks. Identify specific classroom examples that illustrate that effort.

Kingore, B. (2007). *Reaching All Learners.* Austin, TX: Professional Associates Publishing.

26. Integrate process engagement time and closure because they are vital to achievement. It may seem that there is not enough time for process engagement, but finishing the lesson may not insure as much retention as finishing the process. Process engagement and closure are important to enable students to link and connect learning to prior knowledge.

27. Challenge advanced students to integrate abstract thinking, complexity, and depth in most responses.

28. Encourage students to think aloud when problem solving or processing complex information to make the processes clearer. Expect students to use the specific labels: compare, analyze, evaluate, and synthesize.

29. Involve students in using concept mapping to convey understanding of concept relationships.

30. Address issues and ethical concerns related to the topic of study when appropriate with the age group or maturity level of the students. Issue discussions elevate the level of thinking, encourage personal reactions to the information, and increase memory.

31. Keep flexible groups small. Groups of two to four require that more students be on task. Groups of five or six often result in some students doing more of the work.

RESPECT AND RAPPORT

32. Respect students as individuals. The more we respect and respond positively to students as individuals, the more likely they are to respect and respond positively to our learning objectives.

33. Use students' first names more than collective nouns to accent that all students are valued as individuals.

34. Show recognition of individuals as students arrive through eye contact, positive nonverbal responses, and first names.

35. Encourage students to challenge each other's reasoning but respect the person.

36. Demonstrate respect for other adults and students. Vocalize their possible viewpoint if it is different from yours. This response models how we want student to respect and respond to others.

LEARNING TASKS AND PRODUCTS

37. Provide product options to empower students with choice, motivate excellence, and require them to plan and organize. Learning options enable students to select replacement tasks with less teacher planning.

38. Post a template of product options for special need students or for young learners. Add specific tasks over time as the class reaches independence in

Kingore, B. (2007). *Reaching All Learners.* Austin, TX: Professional Associates Publishing.

the task. This developmental process enables students to concretely see that they now know how to accomplish more than when the school year began.

39. Incorporate a wide range of nonfiction materials reflecting the interests and varied reading levels of students. Many students are more engaged in reading when they are learning about a topic of personal interest. A media specialist or librarian is a valued resource when accessing these materials.

40. Make available well-crafted biographies and autobiographies at students' reading ability levels. Students make personal connections to the life models provided by this genre.

41. Provide books with characters to which students can relate.

42. Furnish a variety of stuffed animals or similar creatures to add comfort and interest at selected times, particularly with primary and elementary students. Children enjoy these props and want to use them frequently.
    • Let children select an animal to hold as they read silently.
    • Display an animal or stuffed figure as a model for drawing.
    • Use the figure to prompt rich description and to model more precise vocabulary to incorporate in descriptive writing.
    • Encourage students to develop a figure and its attributes into a character in a narrative.

• Prompt analogies. *List six ways this _____ is like you.*

WHOLE CLASS AND SMALL GROUP MANAGEMENT

At different times:
✦ The teacher directs whole class instruction,
✦ The teacher facilitates the whole class grouped into small groups,
✦ Some students are directly instructed by the teacher in a small group, and
✦ Some students work without direct teacher instruction in small groups or on independent tasks.

Guidelines for when the teacher facilitates the whole class grouped into small groups

43. Communicate high expectations. Believe that students will do well because what you expect and seek you will usually find. Expect to see students learning and vocalize that to them. Set a goal of high expectations as a learning experience begins. *I am eager to see your exit tickets at the end of this lesson and find out from you the new ideas you have learned.*

44. Post a schedule so students know what to expect throughout the week.

45. Be visible and circulate about, as proximity is an important motivator. Avoid a set pattern of movement. Move in response to observations and students' requests for help.

Kingore, B. (2007). *Reaching All Learners*. Austin, TX: Professional Associates Publishing.

46. Model a behavior such as peer editing with a student, and then, prompt discussions by asking a student observer: *What did you notice?*

47. Recognize and regularly reinforce the behaviors you want to see. Verbal acknowledgements, nonverbal smiles or winks, and positive quick notes or written sticky notes handed to a student are all reinforcements that are easily shared.

48. Use eye contact as a management tool. Establish eye contact and study a student or group for a short time.

49. Write notes. As students work in groups, walk around the room carrying a notepad or checklist to take notes and assess as students work. Some students are more motivated to stay on task because they are not sure what you are writing. Also, carry sticky-notes to reinforce effort and provide encouragement through a note of something positive about a student and place it on the desk while walking by.

50. Maintain a quiet, calm voice. Bend close to whisper to some students occasionally a positive or corrective response as needed. Varying the responses avoids the potential stigma of the teacher attending only to negative behaviors.

51. Announce when groups are working on a similar task: *You may use anything you hear from another group.* Usually groups become very quiet to prevent others hearing their ideas.

52. Develop and implement nonverbal signals for quiet or closure. For example, a remote control for a CD player is an effective tool. Simply begin a musical selection to signal students that they have three minutes to finish and be back in their seats.

Guidelines for when students work without direct teacher instruction in small groups or on independent tasks.

53. Convey to students a specific purpose, product, and audience for the fruits of their labor.

54. Communicate expectations and model them as needed so all students know what is expected.

55. Make students' self-assessment a requirement. Provide an assessment tool or require a written record of how they met expectations. Self-assessment increases students' concern for quality and can increase their levels of achievement (Marzano, 2000).

56. Remember the value of novelty. Occasionally, try innovative tasks, unexpected materials, combining instruction with another class to freshen enthusiasm for group tasks, and unusual locations, such as working outside or in the cafeteria.

57. Vary the size of a group as appropriate. The change may be refreshing and typically results in some different members in a group.

Kingore, B. (2007). *Reaching All Learners.* Austin, TX: Professional Associates Publishing.

58. Avoid competitions where only one group wins, as that makes everyone else a loser. Many students feel less motivated to make an effort when they are less sure of winning.

59. Use competition only to motivate personal best and focus on how students are changing and learning. *Today, your challenge is to match or increase the number of effective ideas your group produced last time.* Each team graphs their results using a group behavior or learning behavior rubric. The goal is to strive for consistency and gains.

60. Design each group-learning task at a level that is appropriate to challenge but ensures success. Don't risk frustrating learners or planting the thought that they cannot do well enough to learn.

61. Plan the length of the group task so completion is likely. Group tasks need to be short enough to be interesting, short enough to be realistically completed, but long enough to be important learning experiences.

62. Consider how to respond to partial completions, particularly when an individual or the group largely works on task. For example, ask the student(s) to write an *In Progress* note (Figure 3.1) to set a goal for what to do next.

63. Select students to share information about their group work. Randomly determine who shares information for the group.
    - Ask each group to number off. Then, someone toss a die to determine the number of the person who is to share.
    - Draw a name from a set of name cards arranged by groups.
    - State a category such as: *Who is wearing the most white,* or *Who has*

• **Figure 3.1** •

In Progress

TASK _____

I completed:

Next, I plan:

Kingore, B. (2007). *Reaching All Learners.* Austin, TX: Professional Associates Publishing.

the smallest quantity of letters in their last name? (Be sensitive to avoid potentially negative categories.)

SUGGESTIONS FOR WHEN A PROBLEM OCCURS

64. Involve students in seeking solutions and increasing ownership in classroom operation.

65. Facilitate class meetings and discussions to identify the problem and ponder what can be done to overcome it. Elicit students' suggestions.

66. Role-play problems and solutions. As an engaging switch, the teacher role-plays performing in a learning situation. Students watch and offer suggestions to increase productivity and improve what is being done incorrectly.

67. Use brainwriting to actively involve all students in addressing the potential solutions.

68. Acknowledge mistakes without being too self-critical. A teacher's response models how to handle errors while establishing the position that everyone makes mistakes.

69. Avoid power struggles in front of peers. Avoid stand-offs.

70. Redirect behavior with staccato conversations. Students recognize when adults obsess about a problem or an observed behavior. Increase attention with very brief statements or suggestions. Preplan how to make a point succinctly because less is often more effective and remembered.

71. Practice wait-time. Before reacting or overreacting to a problem, contemplate: *How much does it matter* or *what difference does it make?* Pause to consider a response before reacting.

72. Redirect thinking. Before responding to a situation perceived as negative, brainstorm two or three positive things about it to temper the response. Consider sharing these more positive ramifications with the students while working with them to overcome the problem. *I like your friendship and how closely you work together, but I am concerned about _____.*

73. Move to a potential problem area or situation to quietly defuse it before it escalates. Elicit students' responsibility for their behaviors by first posing questions rather than issuing directives. *What can you do here to help?*

74. Use a perspective log to elicit a student's view of disruptive behavior and a plan for change. When a classroom problem occurs, the student writes in a log her perspective of the situation, one good thing about it, and one or two ways to improve it. The short writing task also serves as a cooling down time.

Kingore, B. (2007). *Reaching All Learners.* Austin, TX: Professional Associates Publishing.

CHAPTER FOUR:
THE TEACHING PALETTE–40 STRATEGIES FOR DIFFERENTIATING INSTRUCTION

Like the board used by painters for holding and mixing colors, teachers need a palette of strategies to select and combine as they differentiate instruction. These strategies remind experienced teachers of techniques that are interesting, effective ways to increase students' achievement and infuse colorful learning experiences for all members of the classroom.

This teaching palette of strategies is organized alphabetically for easy access and blends learning experiences, techniques, skill applications, and modality applications across content areas and grade levels. Some of the strategies require minimum reading and writing skills to promote success for younger students, special-need learners, and English language learners. Use the elements of tiered instruction to tier the complexity level of applications for any of the strategies to better match student populations.

Kingore, B. (2007). *Reaching All Learners.* Austin, TX: Professional Associates Publishing.

3-2-1

Purpose

* Process engagement
* Written and visual-spatial skills
* Informal assessment
* Closure
* Communication with home

Grouping Options

☐ Whole class   ☐ Mixed-readiness groups
☐ Similar-readiness groups   ☐ Trios or pairs   ☑ Individual

What is it?

At the end of a lesson or at the end of the day, provide students with a copy of the 3-2-1 template (Figure 4.1) to assess their level of understanding and reactions to the learning opportunities. It incorporates a visual prompt to engage visual/spatial learners as well. The completed 3-2-1 is taken home to communicate with the family about the day's learning.

Applications

Students write brief responses to the 3-2-1 prompts stated by the teacher, and add quick illustrations or symbols as time allows or as students' needs dictate. Different prompts are used at different times for variety and effectiveness. As students write, the teacher circulates to observe and note students' responses and levels of information. For two minutes following the 3-2-1, students pair and share their responses with a classmate for closure.

Students take their 3-2-1 responses home as a communication device so family members have a more specific discussion prompt. A parent can read the 3-2-1 and ask about specific content instead of asking: *What did you learn at school today?* The exit ticket,

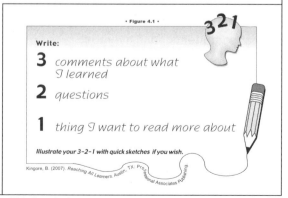

· Figure 4.1 ·

Write:

3 *comments about what I learned*

2 *questions*

1 *thing I want to read more about*

Illustrate your 3-2-1 with quick sketches if you wish.

Kingore, B. (2007). *Reaching All Learners.* Austin, TX: Professional Associates Publishing.

Kingore, B. (2007). *Reaching All Learners.* Austin, TX: Professional Associates Publishing.

another strategy on the teaching palette, provides additional variations and related ideas for process engagement and home communication.

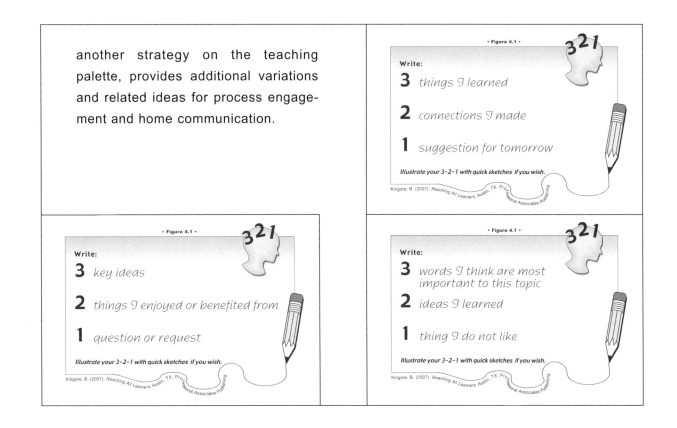

• Figure 4.1 •

Write:

3 things I learned

2 connections I made

1 suggestion for tomorrow

Illustrate your 3-2-1 with quick sketches if you wish.

Kingore, B. (2007). *Reaching All Learners.* Austin, TX: Professional Associates Publishing.

• Figure 4.1 •

Write:

3 key ideas

2 things I enjoyed or benefited from

1 question or request

Illustrate your 3-2-1 with quick sketches if you wish.

Kingore, B. (2007). *Reaching All Learners.* Austin, TX: Professional Associates Publishing.

• Figure 4.1 •

Write:

3 words I think are most important to this topic

2 ideas I learned

1 thing I do not like

Illustrate your 3-2-1 with quick sketches if you wish.

Kingore, B. (2007). *Reaching All Learners.* Austin, TX: Professional Associates Publishing.

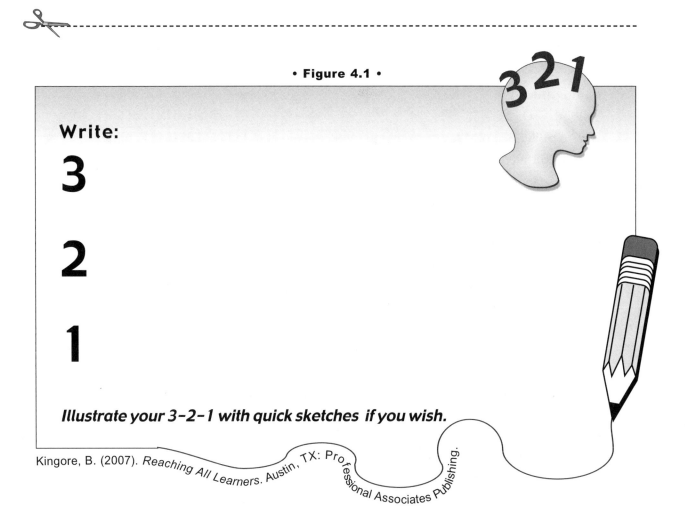

• **Figure 4.1** •

Write:

3

2

1

Illustrate your 3-2-1 with quick sketches if you wish.

Kingore, B. (2007). *Reaching All Learners. Austin, TX: Professional Associates Publishing.*

A & E CARD (ASSESSMENT AND EVALUATION CARD)

Purpose

- Assessment
- Evaluation
- Flexible grouping
- Closure

Grouping Options

- ☐ Whole class   ☐ Mixed-readiness groups
- ☐ Similar-readiness groups   ☐ Trios or pairs   ☑ Individual

What is it?

The A & E card is a strategy to assess students' understanding of a concept or skill. Determine short-answer questions related to learning objectives. Students respond to the questions on an A & E card (Figure 4.2), and the teacher uses the results to sort students into instructional groups.

Applications

At the end of class, post one to three questions or tasks to assess a curriculum objective or learning standard and provide a blank index card or a printed template for students' short answer responses. Half sheets of paper or four-by-six-inch index cards work best for students' writing space and the teacher's ease in reviewing or sorting based upon assessed needs. The process requires four to eight minutes and incorporates short answer prompts such as those on the following pages.

This is a variation of exit tickets that more specifically evaluates the students' understanding of a concept or skill. This assessment tool is used about once a week or at a juncture of learning when a teacher wants feedback about the students' level of understanding to guide teaching and grouping decisions.

Using A & E cards results in instructional, similar-readiness groups. The objective is to match instruction to students' most appropriate challenge level.

Kingore, B. (2007). *Reaching All Learners.* Austin, TX: Professional Associates Publishing.

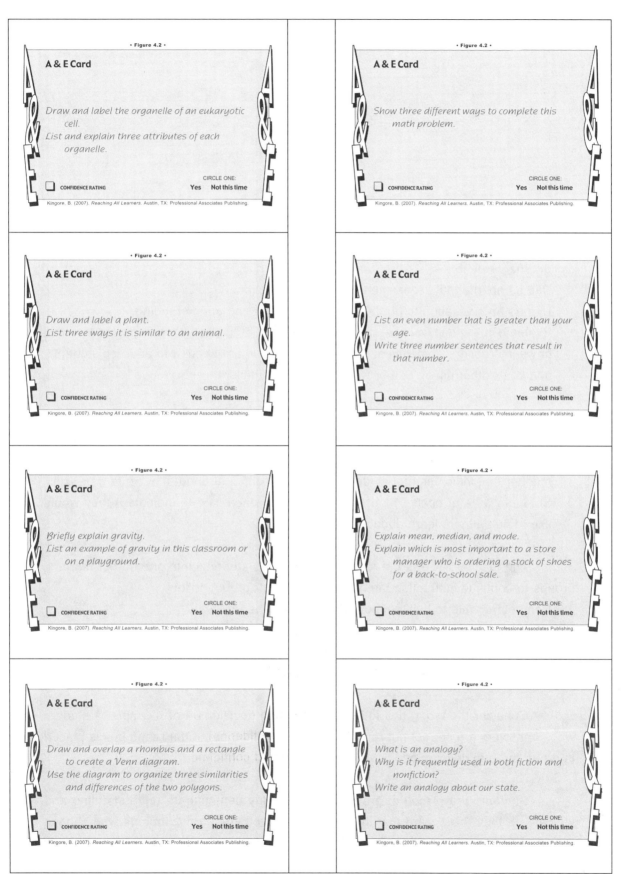

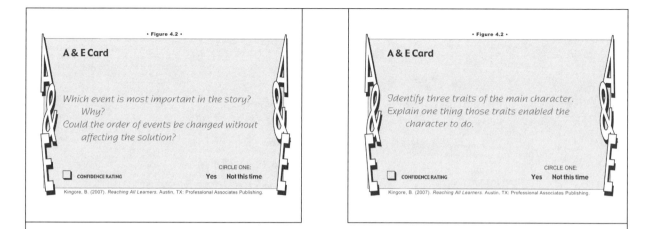

Collect the cards to:

• Use as an informal assessment to guide instruction.

• Use as an evaluation to grade daily participation and understanding.

• Evaluate the quality of the responses and sort students into groups for the next day's instruction. Sometimes, three or four groups are needed to address students' needs. At other times, one or two groups are sufficient.

Two additions to the card increase the value of this strategy.

1. Students record a *1* to *3* or *1* to *5* in the confidence box to self-assess their confidence in their understanding. A *1* indicates a low confidence continuing to the highest number that indicates that students feel quite confident about this content or skill.

2. Students write or circle *Yes* or *Not this time* on each card to indicate if they would like to help others learn about this topic.

The teacher reviews the responses and sorts students into one of four learning groups to continue instruction the next day. The four groups follow.

1. Competent; able to help support others as they learn

2. Competent; needs extensions

3. Basic understanding; needs guided practice

4. Confused or inaccurate; needs reteaching and clarification

Consider the rating box to finalize grouping decisions. For example, a student whose answers are correct but records a *1* (low confidence) in the rating box is placed in group three to develop additional background and confidence.

Students are placed in group one when they demonstrate understanding and indicate on their A & E card that they want to help others learn. Students who choose to help others are more likely to be effective in the task. It is not negative for students to indicate *Not this time*. Students deserve the right for time to work to extend their own learning.

When multiple students are in group one, the teacher pairs a student from group one and group three by matching students for productivity. Structure a task for the pairs to do. (Students elect to facilitate; they are not responsible for developing the lesson.) Students in group two are given interesting extension tasks or personal applications of the topic to complete independently. The teacher directs the instruction of the students in group four. This process results in flexible groups, differentiated by readiness. The teacher has a smaller group of students to more effectively customize reteaching needs.

• **Figure 4.2** •

A & E Card

☐ **CONFIDENCE RATING**

CIRCLE ONE:

Yes **Not this time**

Kingore, B. (2007). *Reaching All Learners*. Austin, TX: Professional Associates Publishing.

ANALOGIES

yellow ➤➤

as

red ➤➤

Purpose
- Relating and integrating information
- Inference
- High-level thinking
- Assessing
- Conceptual understanding

Grouping Options
☑ Whole class   ☑ Mixed-readiness groups
☑ Similar-readiness groups   ☑ Trios or pairs   ☑ Individual

What is it?

Analogies are a more complex format for relating similarities and differences—the most significant strategy for increasing student achievement (Marzano, 2001). They connect two seemingly unrelated items or ideas to create a relationship. Forming analogies is a significant factor in identifying understanding as students must understand both objects well to create a relationship.

Applications

Analogies can be oral or written and prove effective with all age groups. They aid long-term memory as they enable students to relate chunks of information instead of focus on memorizing facts. To promote achievement and long-term learning, analogies are most effective when they are content specific and progress from teacher developed to student created.

With young children, prompt analogous thinking by asking students to orally respond to how a random item relates to the current topic of study. Some teachers call this *linking thinking* as they prompt students' connections to content. Encouraging multiple responses increases the likelihood of more in-depth thinking and models that there is more than one potentially correct answer. Open-ended, multiple-response techniques promote students' intellectual risk-taking during class discussions.
- *How is this bottle of water like our bodies?*
- *How is this flashlight like an early explorer?*
- *How is the shuttle like the Earth?*

Kingore, B. (2007). *Reaching All Learners.* Austin, TX: Professional Associates Publishing.

DIRECT ANALOGIES

Direct analogies may be written or orally shared as an effective review and closure technique. To assess understanding and promote memory, the teacher forms incomplete analogies about the topic for students to discuss and then share their best answers. Additionally, pairs or trios of students can create analogies for other students to complete as a closure activity.

* *A triangle is to three as a hexagon is to _____.*
* *E. L. Konigsburg is to contemporary realistic fiction as Elizabeth George Speare is to _____.*
* *The wall of China is to isolationism as a _____ in _____ is to Manifest Destiny.*

Direct analogies are thought-provoking tools to tease out inferences. For example, ask students to pose and explain an analogy expressing how the historical explorer being studied is like a part of the body or how a scientist is like an item in the laboratory.

PERSONAL ANALOGIES

Personal analogies are also appropriate applications to content. With a personal analogy, students relate themselves to the object or topic.

* *I am like this main character when _____.*
* *If I were an early explorer, I would be _____ because _____.*
* *If I were an ocean animal, I would not want to be a _____ because _____.*

Kingore, B. (2007). *Reaching All Learners.* Austin, TX: Professional Associates Publishing.

ANALYZE IT

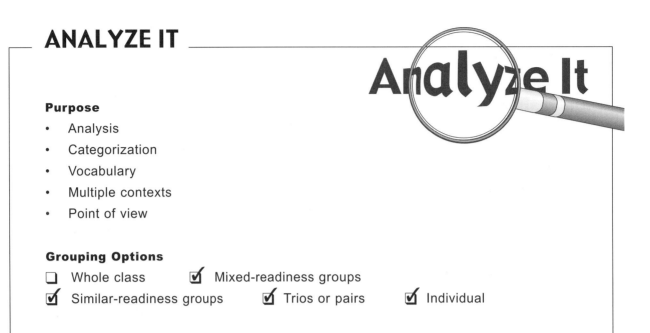

Purpose

• Analysis
• Categorization
• Vocabulary
• Multiple contexts
• Point of view

Grouping Options

☐ Whole class   ☑ Mixed-readiness groups
☑ Similar-readiness groups   ☑ Trios or pairs   ☑ Individual

What is it?

Analyze It uses a simple graphic organizer to prompt analysis of a concept, topic, or skill through multiple contexts.

Applications

Students use the template in Figure 4.4 or fold a paper into four boxes. For a specified topic, the teacher designates four categories that students record as labels for the boxes on their paper. They then analyze the topic, concept, or skill by organizing information in each category. Students are encouraged to use words, phrases, and sketches as means to share content.

Many different categories are possible, and they should vary with the topic being studied. Select the categories that prompt the students' analysis of the most significant aspects of the topic. For example, it the task involved analyzing a novel, effective categories could be point of view, issues, relationships, and solutions. To analyze a math operation, however, the categories of attributes, symbols, examples, and non-examples are more applicable. Consider the categories in Figure 4.3 for additional possibilities and use them with Figure 4.4

The strategy integrates high-level thinking, uses multiple modes of learning, and encourages specific vocabulary related to the topic. Requiring students to investigate a skill or concept through multiple contexts increases comprehension.

Kingore, B. (2007). *Reaching All Learners.* Austin, TX: Professional Associates Publishing.

• **Figure 4.3** •
Analyze It: Sample Categories

- Adjectives
- Analogy
- Associations
- Attributes
- Causes
- Comparisons
- Connections
- Descriptions
- Design
- Essential characteristics
- Events
- Examples
- Influences

- Issues
- Needs
- Nonessential characteristics
- Non-examples
- Nouns
- Opinions
- Patterns
- People
- Perspective
- Places
- Problems
- Questions
- Relationships

- Solutions
- Stereotypes
- Summary
- Symbols
- Terminology

- Tools
- Utility
- Values
- Verbs

• Figure 4.4 •

Analyze It!

TOPIC _Equivalent fractions_

• _Attributes_	• _Terminology_
Fractions that have the same value; some equivalent fractions can be reduced; a quotient of numbers	Denominator–bottom number; the total number of parts Numerator–top number; how many parts I have

• _Examples_	• _Non-examples_
$\frac{1}{3}$ $\frac{2}{6}$ $\frac{3}{9}$ $\frac{100}{300}$	$\frac{3}{8}$ $\frac{1}{17}$ $\frac{1}{2}$ $\frac{100}{200}$

Kingore, B. (2007). *Reaching All Learners.* Austin, TX: Professional Associates Publishing.

• **Figure 4.4** •

Analyze It!

TOPIC _____

• _____	• _____
• _____	• _____

Kingore, B. (2007). *Reaching All Learners.* Austin, TX: Professional Associates Publishing.

BACKGROUND GROUP

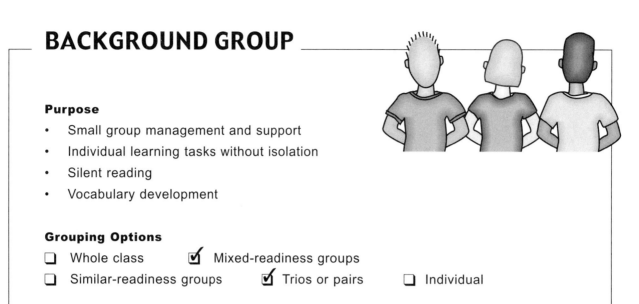

Purpose

* Small group management and support
* Individual learning tasks without isolation
* Silent reading
* Vocabulary development

Grouping Options

☐ Whole class   ☑ Mixed-readiness groups

☐ Similar-readiness groups   ☑ Trios or pairs   ☐ Individual

What is it?

A background group is typically a mixed-readiness group sitting together while the students actually work individually. It is parallel learning–working side by side but not interacting to complete the learning task. The teacher determines group membership and sets an academic purpose for each member, such as vocabulary development.

Applications

This strategy is a productive choice for sustained silent reading applications. Since silent reading is significantly related to building academic vocabularies (ASCD, 2006), teachers seek ways to integrate silent reading with simple management techniques that increase on-task behavior.

A small group of students is organized with their backs to the class but in close proximity to the teacher who is involved in direct instruction with

Kingore, B. (2007). *Reaching All Learners.* Austin, TX: Professional Associates Publishing.

another group of students. A third-grader called it *back-around reading* as she misheard the term but labeled the task appropriately. The intent is for all of the students to have their backs to other activities and thus limit their distractions. The teacher is seated to view all of the students when working directly with a small instructional group.

The strategy is an advantage for students who benefit from the movement and variety of working away from their usual desk or table. The proximity to the teacher enables some students to focus more on their learning tasks with less distractions. The teacher can also more quickly help or coach during transition moments.

To maximize the benefits of the strategy, schedule three minutes at the end of the task for the background group to share ideas from their reading. The teacher moves into the group to listen and encourage as students share before they move out of the group.

Students in a middle school social studies class read historical fiction in their background groups. Their reading adds personal interest and depth to classroom discussions as they compare historical fiction details with the historical period of current study.

An elementary teacher adds novelty to the technique by inviting children to bring a prop to their background group. The prop must be something related to what they are reading, and students are encouraged to explain the relationship. Some students select literal props, such as a baseball when reading a sports story. Others demonstrate more abstract thinking with selections, such as a family photograph to represent the character's search for belonging.

Kingore, B. (2007). *Reaching All Learners.* Austin, TX: Professional Associates Publishing.

BEFORE-AFTER-SUPPORT

Purpose
- Activate background knowledge
- Preassess
- Mental engagement
- Analysis
- Substantiation

Grouping Options
- ☐ Whole class
- ☑ Mixed-readiness groups
- ☑ Similar-readiness groups
- ☑ Trios or pairs
- ☑ Individual

What is it?

Before-after-support is an anticipation guide to activate students' background knowledge and interest in a topic while challenging them to substantiate their information. Students indicate whether they agree or disagree to a series of statements before and after they read.

Applications

This strategy, a variation of an anticipation guide (Readence, Bean, & Baldwin, 1989), elicits students' responses before they begin reading, asks them to revisit their responses after reading, and adds the requirement that students support their final opinions by noting references. Prepare four to eight statements about the concepts to be learned in an upcoming topic of study. Ask students to write whether they agree or disagree

• Figure 4.5 •

Before-After-Support   TOPIC _Immigration_

RESOURCES _Textbook, Video, and Harris' New Americans_

Before A/D	Mark if you agree (A) or disagree (D) before and after you research each statement.	After A/D	Support page
D	1. Immigration is more of an issue in the USA today than ever before.	A	T:36, H:50
A	2. People immigrate to the USA for freedom.	A	V
A	3. Aliens are people living in the USA illegally.	D	H:5, V
D	4. The Immigration Bureau sets different yearly quotas for each country to control the number of people allowed to enter the USA from that country.	A	T:39
D	5. More people enter the U.S. legally than illegally.	A	H:94

Kingore, B. (2007). *Reaching All Learners.* Austin, TX: Professional Associates Publishing.

with each statement before they begin the study and after they have read related information. Design statements to assess prior knowledge, cause students to think at higher levels about the content, and include both true information and misconceptions.

The template in Figure 4.5 provides a means of organizing this strategy. Use before-after-support as an introduction to a topic of study that involves opinions or issues. Students respond to a list of statements about the topic by designating if they agree or disagree. Psychologically, the act of recording their opinion increases their interest in following through and learning about the topic. The teacher reviews their responses to assess background knowledge.

As their study progresses, students collect and substantiate data relating to each point. For closure, students revisit their responses, state whether they now agree or disagree, and support their conclusions with data from their reading and discussions. The teacher can assess changes in students' misconceptions and the depth of their information by their elaboration to explain their conclusions.

• **Figure 4.5** •

Before-After-Support

TOPIC _____

RESOURCES _____

Before A/D	Mark if you agree (A) or disagree (D) before and after you research each statement.	After A/D	Support page

Kingore, B. (2007). *Reaching All Learners.* Austin, TX: Professional Associates Publishing.

BRAINWRITING

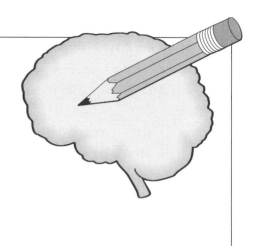

Purpose
- Active participation in brainstorming tasks
- Generate multiple content-related Ideas
- Classification
- Analysis
- Compare and contrast

Grouping Options
☐ Whole class   ☑ Mixed-readiness groups
☑ Similar-readiness groups   ☑ Trios or pairs   ☐ Individual

What is it?

Brainwriting (Shade & Garrett, 2002) is a written variation of brainstorming that increases mental engagement for all students. The written products that result invite students to compare and contrast concepts related to the topic.

Applications

A group of three to five students is organized around a table or set of desks. Each person in the group has a brainwriting sheet; an extra copy is placed in the middle of the table. Students can use the template provided in figure 4.6 or fold plain paper into four boxes and draw a rectangle in the middle to organize the sheet. The activity works best with a small group of students so there is a rich pool of ideas in a manageable interactive group.

For a current topic of study, the teacher selects the categories that prompt the students' greatest analysis of the topic, such as the following.

• Adjectives	• Needs	• Relationships	• Traits
• Attributes	• Nouns	• Solutions	• Verbs
• Causes	• People	• Stereotypes	
• Events	• Places	• Symbols	
• Issues	• Problems	• Tools	

After recording the topic at the top of the paper, students write the subtopic in the middle of their brainwriting sheet. Then, label each box surrounding the topic with a category designated by the teacher.

Kingore, B. (2007). *Reaching All Learners.* Austin, TX: Professional Associates Publishing.

When the brainwriting begins, each student writes an idea in one of the spaces provided, exchanges that sheet for the one in the middle of the table, writes a different idea on the new sheet, and then exchanges again. This brainwriting process continues for three or four minutes or until all the sheets are filled.

Each group then prepares to share and compare information with the class. This information signals the concepts that are considered to be more significant to most of the class and reveals any misconceptions that need to be addressed. The result is a rich resource for summarization or expanded writing about the topic.

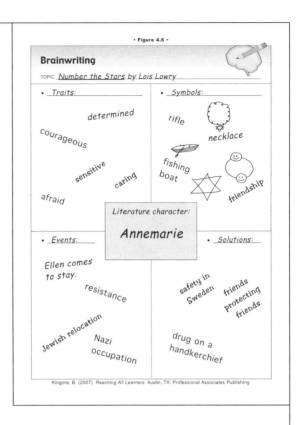

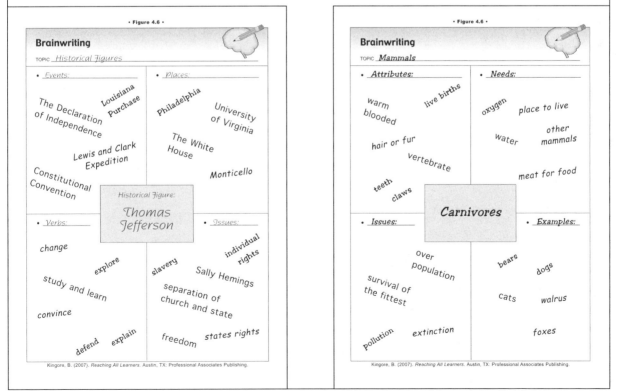

Kingore, B. (2007). *Reaching All Learners.* Austin, TX: Professional Associates Publishing.

• **Figure 4.6** •

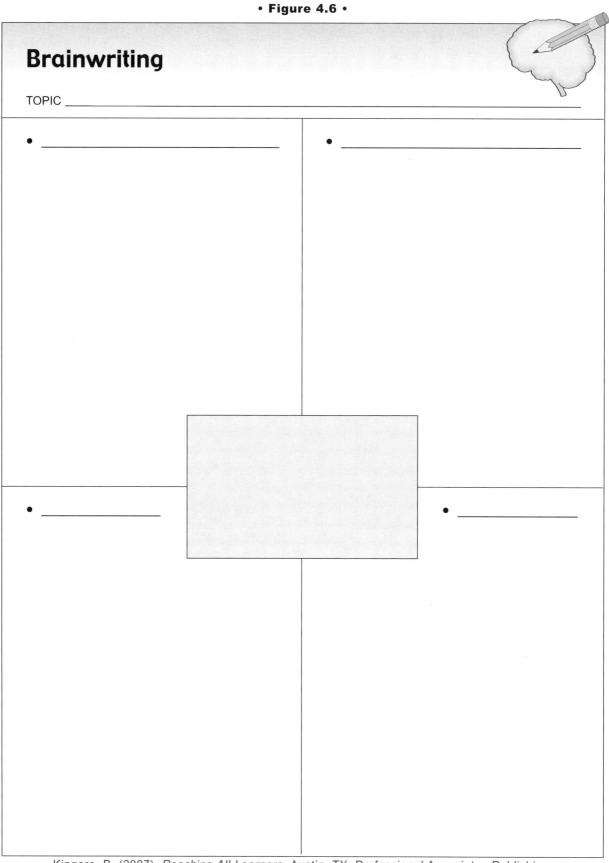

Brainwriting

TOPIC _____

- _____

- _____

- _____

- _____

Kingore, B. (2007). *Reaching All Learners.* Austin, TX: Professional Associates Publishing.

BUDDIES

Purpose
• Peer tutoring
• One-to-one skill practice and extension
• Small group management
• Peer interaction
• Review

Grouping Options
☐ Whole class ☐ Mixed-readiness groups
☐ Similar-readiness groups ☑ Trios or pairs ☐ Individual

What is it?

Buddies are pairs or trios of students within a class or students from more than one class helping one another in a learning task.

Applications

Students know their teacher is there to help them, but they also need to view their classmates as sources of assistance. Students working together build class colleagueship and the results often benefit both students as one helps another clarify an idea or process.

PEER TUTORS

Pair students by compatibility, readiness, needs, and/or interests. Most often, one able or older student is paired with a student who would benefit from one-to-one guided practice to refine skills. The teacher plans the learning task, and buddies work together for ten to twenty minutes to complete the task.

Buddies can be scheduled once a week or more as needed. Younger or struggling students benefit from the individual attention and practice. Older or able students benefit from the self-concept boost of being able to help someone as they practice and refine skills. ELL students benefit from working with a bilingual buddy.

Kingore, B. (2007). *Reaching All Learners.* Austin, TX: Professional Associates Publishing.

Older or Able Students	Younger or Struggling Students
• Integrating basic skills	• Practicing basic skills
• Communication skills	• Communication skills
• Social skills	• Social skills
• High-level thinking	• High-level thinking
• Flexibility in thought and process	• Reading/writing model
• Time management	• Individual attention
• Self-esteem: *Someone needs my help*.	• Self-esteem: *Someone likes to work with me*.
• Planning	
• Organizational skills	
• Responsibility	

STUDY BUDDY

Vary buddy interactions so they are not exclusively a peer tutor or remedial time.

• Advanced learners within a class or across classes can sometimes work together as buddies to encourage greater complexity and challenge in their work.

• Two students with a similar interest in a topic can work together to continue their learning.

• An able and a struggling student, in addition to peer tutoring for skill practice, can sometimes read together, work together on problem solving, brainstorm, or draw and complete art projects together.

As a review technique, teachers schedule study-buddy times for the whole class or as a flexible group task while the teacher completes a guided lesson with some students. Each student selects a study buddy, and they work quietly together for ten or more minutes to review material or ask each other questions about the material. When the buddies are productive, the process is easily repeated as appropriate. When the buddies are not productive, the teacher selects the pairs the next time.

BUDDY WRITTEN REQUESTS

As an authentic writing experience, students complete written notes requesting help from either a peer tutor or a study buddy. Figure 4.7 on the next page enables the buddy to plan and be more prepared to help.

Kingore, B. (2007). *Reaching All Learners.* Austin, TX: Professional Associates Publishing.

COOPERATIVE DRAWING

This cooperative drawing task is an effective way to initiate a class discussion of working respectfully with buddies.

Group the class in pairs with one large piece of paper for each pair to share. Each student selects one crayon or marker and uses that color to write his/her name on the back of the paper. Set a timer for five minutes and ask the pairs to draw together until time is up. They may not get another color or exchange colors with their partner.

- Ask each pair of students to engage in comparative thinking by writing two ways their art is similar and two ways it is different from one another. Discuss style and individuality. Develop the idea that different does not necessarily mean better or worse.

- Discuss ways that students cooperated (worked well together), collaborated (developed one picture together), or worked independently (produced different pictures on different parts of the paper). *Did any pair overlap their two colors to create a third color?* Accent that there are many ways to work well together.

• **Figure 4.7** •

Request for Help

Dear _____,

I need help with:

I do not understand:

I have this question:

Sincerely,

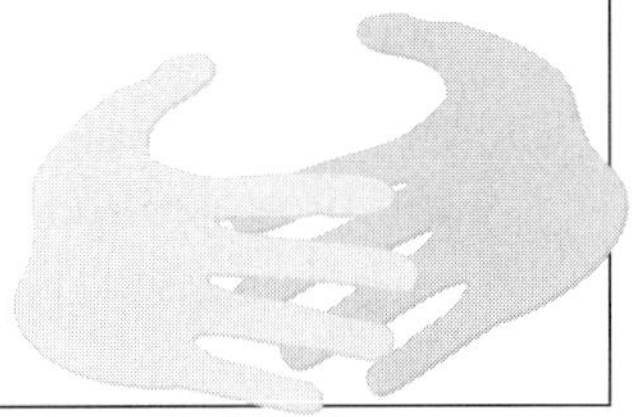

_____

Kingore, B. (2007). *Reaching All Learners.* Austin, TX: Professional Associates Publishing.

CATEGORY GRID

Category

Purpose

- Analyzing and comparing attributes
- Visual-spatial-kinesthetic task
- Assessment and evaluation
- Classification
- Conceptual understanding

Grouping Options

- [ ] Whole class
- [x] Mixed-readiness groups
- [x] Similar-readiness groups
- [x] Trios or pairs
- [x] Individual

What is it?

A category grid is a graphic organizer that students create to structure information in a comparative form for analyzing the attributes or major characteristics of a topic or concept.

Applications

On chart or butcher paper, students draw the grid with two to four inch spaces for writing responses. For a given topic, the subparts or examples are written down the column on the left and attributes are listed across the row at the top. In small groups or as individuals, the students complete the grid by recording written or illustrated responses in each cell.

Category grids are similar to analysis grids (Kingore, 1999), but provide space for written responses and elaboration by students as they organize content relationships. The main focus is the analysis and comparison of the significant attributes of a topic. It is very effective as a culminating task requiring students to categorize

Consumer Goods	Can be eaten	Can be worn	Can be used in the classroom
25¢	A piece of candy Pack of cheese or peanut butter crackers	Toy ring, bracelet, or necklace Washable tattoo Sticker	Pencil Pen Eraser Paperback folder
$1.00	Bag of chips Bag of cookies	Socks Hair ribbons or bows Barrettes	Supply box Glue Scissors Ruler Crayons Computer disk
$5.00	Value meal Meat	Shirt Sweater Scarf Earrings	Watercolor set Stapler Large notebook Calendar

and organize the significant parts of the whole concept or topic. When completed in pairs or small groups, extensive discussion ensues as students complete the task.

Kingore, B. (2007). *Reaching All Learners.* Austin, TX: Professional Associates Publishing.

This discussion encourages them to define and refine their thinking.

Extend the value of category grids through the following tasks.

- Discuss the similarities and differences observed on the completed grid.
- Increase the analysis required by challenging students to expand the grid with another attribute or another item to compare.
- Instead of selecting the attributes and examples for students to analyze, challenge students to discuss the topic and determine which attributes and examples to include on the grid. Have students work in small groups to determine attributes and examples; then, they meet as a whole class to compare and discuss the different choices.
- Use the grid as a pre- or posttest to evaluate students' accuracy and depth of the information.

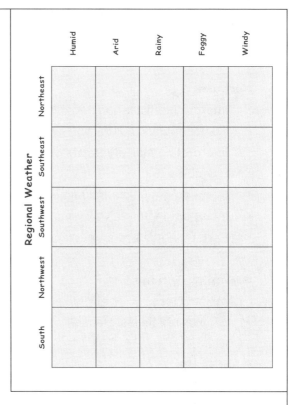

States of Matter

	Atoms	When heated	When cooled
Solid	Very close together	Turns into a liquid	No change
Liquid	Separated by a small distance	Turns into a gas	Turns into a solid
Gas	Far apart	No change	Turns into a liquid

Kingore, B. (2007). *Reaching All Learners.* Austin, TX: Professional Associates Publishing.

CHORAL READING

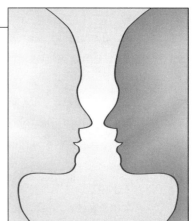

Purpose

*   Interpreting fiction and nonfiction
*   Comparing and contrasting categories of information
*   Interpreting multiple points of view
*   Fluency
*   Integrating multiple modalities
*   Incorporating creative dramatics
*   Performing before an audience

Grouping Options

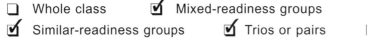

☐ Whole class   ☑ Mixed-readiness groups

☑ Similar-readiness groups   ☑ Trios or pairs   ☐ Individual

What is it?

Choral reading is a group of students sharing the experience of reading aloud text that is organized into parts or sections.

Applications

Increase interest in choral reading by sharing and performing selections from Fleischman's *Joyful Noise: Poems for Two Voices* or Hobberman's *You Read to Me, I'll Read to You*. Rather than memorization, the emphasis is on communication and the creative interpretation of the literature as students expressively read their parts. Students usually just sit or stand to read their lines, but simple movements or actions can be incorporated if it helps children have more fun with their production.

All children can participate successfully in choral reading. Reading in teams provides support for struggling readers, ELL, or introspective learners. Repeated performances encourage fluency and confidence. Parts can be expanded to challenge advanced learners or carefully developed to meet the needs of ELL or at-risk learners. Multiple languages can even be cleverly incorporated into the scripts.

Kingore, B. (2007). *Reaching All Learners.* Austin, TX: Professional Associates Publishing.

CONTENT INTEGRATION

The greatest learning effects of choral reading result when students interpret fiction or nonfiction and write their own scripts. Then, choral reading becomes a content-integrated learning experience involving thinking, reading, writing, listening, and speaking. Students successfully write and perform simple scripts when working in groups of two to four to insure a rich pool of ideas while encouraging active involvement from all students.

COMPARATIVE THINKING AND POINT OF VIEW

Comparison and multiple perspectives are significant skills woven into the Fleischman and Hobberman texts. Challenge students to develop choral readings that compare two concepts, such as living and nonliving, or contrast perspectives, such as the view of the protagonist and the antagonist in the novel they are reading. Incorporating comparison and perspective enables choral reading scripts to be a challenging closure or summary of the topic.

Choral reading is most motivating to students when it is performed. Begin with students informally presenting to one another and quickly move to sharing performances with other classes. Typically, the performance is addictive and motivates students to want to create more scripts.

I am water. I fill the lake.

I am a salmon. I was born in the lake.

The plants and animals need me to live.

My brothers and sisters feed and play with me.

I am their home.

Until it's time to leave.

We rush down the river together and into the sea.

We rush down the river together and into the sea.

I mix with the salt and join the ocean.

I live happily in our new home until it's time to go.

I evaporate and rain

I fight to lay my eggs back into the lake.

back into the lake.

I am a nonliving cycle.

I am a living cycle.

Kingore, B. (2007). *Reaching All Learners.* Austin, TX: Professional Associates Publishing.

VOCABULARY DEVELOPMENT

Use choral reading as a format for building academic vocabulary. Figure 4.8 outlines the basic format for incorporating vocabulary building. The process encourages students to use a dictionary and thesaurus and relate multiple word contexts about the topic.

• Figure 4.8 •
Vocabulary Development and Choral Reading

Steps

1. Students write a sentence that incorporates a simile or metaphor about a topic
2. They organize significant synonyms or adjectives about the topic.
3. They end with a second sentence to conclude the format.

Rattlesnakes

Poisonous snakes are stealth bombers in the underbrush.	*Poisonous snakes are stealth bombers in the underbrush.*
Wriggling	
	Slithering
Sensing	
	Stalking
Constricting like an accordion	
	Moving like a wave
The snake pushes forward to capture its prey and survive.	*The snake pushes forward to capture its prey and survive.*

Kingore, B. (2007). *Reaching All Learners.* Austin, TX: Professional Associates Publishing.

DOCUMENTATION CHART

Purpose

• Inference skills

• Mental engagement when reading

• Advanced organizer for a discussion

• Substantiation

Grouping Options

☐ Whole class   ☐ Mixed-readiness groups
☐ Similar-readiness groups   ☑ Trios or pairs   ☑ Individual

What is it?

A documentation chart is a graphic organizer for fiction or nonfiction that students complete as they read. The intent is give them a reason to carefully read the text and to increase their analysis of significant content. Before reading or as they begin reading, students make inferences about the content and then continue reading to find evidence that substantiates or negates their inferences.

Applications

A documentation chart increases students' active involvement when reading and guides students' preparation for a discussion. Students use the template in Figure 4.9. After experience with the strategy, students can fold paper into thirds, label each column with the headings for a documentation chart, and proceed with the process.

Students bring their completed charts to the discussion to share and compare ideas. Discussions are more lively because students are better prepared and have support for their ideas rather than just engage in arguments.

• Figure 4.9 •

Documentation Chart   Document

TOPIC _Reading_
RESOURCE(S) __More Than Anything Else__
__by Marie Bradby__

Subject	Inference	Supporting Evidence in the Text
Boy-Booker	He is pretty smart.	He wanted to read when others didn't. He learned very quickly.
Blue book	It was probably stolen.	The mother hid it. She wouldn't say where she got it.
News-paper man	He was not raised in the town where Booker lived.	He knew how to read when others did not. He dressed more professionally.

Kingore, B. (2007). *Reaching All Learners.* Austin, TX: Professional Associates Publishing.

Kingore, B. (2007). *Reaching All Learners.* Austin, TX: Professional Associates Publishing.

• Figure 4.9 •

Documentation Chart

Document

TOPIC _____

RESOURCE(S) _____

_____

Subject	Inference	Supporting Evidence in the Text

Kingore, B. (2007). *Reaching All Learners.* Austin, TX: Professional Associates Publishing.

EXIT TICKET

Purpose
- Process engagement
- Informal assessment
- Multiple modalities
- Closure
- Communication with family

Grouping Options
☐ Whole class   ☐ Mixed-readiness groups
☐ Similar-readiness groups   ☐ Trios or pairs   ☑ Individual

What is it?

An exit ticket is a template used at the end of a lesson or at the end of the day to assess students' level of understanding and reactions to learning opportunities. Visual/spatial learners enjoy completing the caricature at the top to communicate their feelings. Depending upon the level and type of prompt, the completed exit ticket can be collected by the teacher or taken home to communicate with the family about the day's learning focus.

Applications

Students write brief responses to the prompts listed on the exit ticket. The process provides a quick assessment response that requires about three minutes response time and another two minutes sharing time at the end of class. As students write, the teacher circulates to observe and note students' responses and levels of information. Students then pair and share their responses with a classmate for closure.

Several examples of prompts for exit tickets are shared on the next page. Figure 4.10 is a blank template for an exit ticket so teachers can customize it to their needs.

Exit tickets are used as a ticket out at the end of a period or day and can be taken home for family communication or collected by the teacher as an informal assessment. The 3-2-1 strategy shared on this teaching palette provides additional variations and related ideas for process engagement and home communication.

Kingore, B. (2007). *Reaching All Learners.* Austin, TX: Professional Associates Publishing.

• Figure 4.10 •

Exit ticket

ASSIGNMENT _____

I feel

Our learning objective was
_____

One thing I did to learn it
_____

Next, I will
_____

Kingore, B. (2007). *Reaching All Learners.* Austin, TX: Professional Associates Publishing.

• Figure 4.10 •

Exit ticket

ASSIGNMENT _____

I feel

Something important I learned
_____

I can use this to
_____

A problem or issue
_____

Kingore, B. (2007). *Reaching All Learners.* Austin, TX: Professional Associates Publishing.

• Figure 4.10 •

Exit ticket

ASSIGNMENT _____

I feel

I worked on
_____

I learned
_____

I wonder/I wish
_____

Kingore, B. (2007). *Reaching All Learners.* Austin, TX: Professional Associates Publishing.

• Figure 4.10 •

Exit ticket

ASSIGNMENT _____

I feel

One thing I accomplished today
_____

What I did to participate
_____

I want to know more about
_____

Kingore, B. (2007). *Reaching All Learners.* Austin, TX: Professional Associates Publishing.

• **Figure 4.10** •

Exit Ticket

ASSIGNMENT _____

I feel

_____

_____

_____

_____

_____

_____

Kingore, B. (2007). *Reaching All Learners.* Austin, TX: Professional Associates Publishing.

FOUR CORNERS

Purpose
- Oral presentations
- Point of view
- Peer audience
- Closure
- Informal assessment

Grouping Options

☐ Whole class ☑ Mixed-readiness groups
☑ Similar-readiness groups ☐ Trios or pairs ☐ Individual

What is it?

Students divide into small groups and get together in or near the parameters of the classroom for sharing information, presentations, or demonstrations. Because four corners are used, students are in smaller groups that encourage active engagement. More students get to benefit from presenting their work with a peer audience in less class time.

Applications

Four corners is an effective application of flexible groups. The groups can be formed randomly or by student choice, depending upon the teacher's objectives. The strategy has multiple values.

- Students have an authentic audience with whom to share their work. Students' motivation for higher achievement increases when there is an authentic audience for their efforts.
- By having four students share at the same time, the use of the class time is more realistic.
- The smaller group size increases the likelihood that students more actively listen to one another.
- Introspective students feel more comfortable when presenting to a small group rather than the whole class.
- The teacher can circulate among the groups writing notes to informally assess and guide future instruction.

Kingore, B. (2007). *Reaching All Learners.* Austin, TX: Professional Associates Publishing.

CLOSURE

Organize the class into four groups to relocate in each corner of the classroom. In each corner, students take turns standing and sharing work with the group.

PRESENTATIONS

As a variation of Donald Graves (1994) author's-chair technique, this application is useful to feature products students have worked on for some time, such as a research project, problem-solving task, artistic response, or written composition. Create a sign for each of the four corners of the room and laminate it for repeated use. Write a topic or student's name on each sign to post in each area as an anticipatory set that provides student recognition. *This corner presents _____.*

OPINION POSITIONS

In each corner, post one of the following laminated cards: *Strongly agree, agree, disagree, strongly disagree.* The cards are written with print sized to be clearly read across the room. Pose a provocative statement related to the topic of study and ask students to relocate to the sign that best matches their response. The groups form and discuss their reactions. After two minutes, the teacher randomly calls on one person from each group to summarize that group's position: *The person in the group who is wearing the most blue will summarize.* As a variation, use only two cards at first to model the process or to accommodate students who would benefit from fewer choices.

MATH DEMONSTRATIONS

Many teachers use the technique of one student completing a math problem in front of the class while everyone else watches. Four corners greatly increases mental engagement and active participation during these demonstrations. In each corner, two or three students work together to demonstrate how to complete a math problem they have prepared to present to a small group. The process takes about ten minutes. If this strategy is used once a week, every student has the opportunity to complete a demonstration every three weeks.

Kingore, B. (2007). *Reaching All Learners.* Austin, TX: Professional Associates Publishing.

GIVE ME FIVE

Purpose

- Flexible and productive thinking
- Informal assessment
- Intellectual risk-taking
- Content depth
- Content connections

Grouping Options

☑ Whole class   ☐ Mixed-readiness groups

☐ Similar-readiness groups   ☐ Trios or pairs   ☑ Individual

What is it?

State a category or problem and prompt multiple responses from students by declaring: *Give me five!* Hold up one hand to signal students to figure out five or more examples or responses to the topic instead of only one answer. Close one finger on the hand as an example is shared.

Applications

Give me five is a simple and instant way to promote multiple responses and greater depth to students' thinking about a concept or skill. Wait time is an important component in this strategy as more depth takes thinking time. Students typically are quick to respond with two or three examples and then slow down as they have to think more about the category. Provide time for students to ponder possibilities if a rich pool of examples is expected. The strategy can be applied to multiple topics and documents that multiple ideas and intellectual risk-taking is valued.

After successful modeling as a whole class, ask students to individually produce five responses to a category or prompt. Follow-up the task with students evaluating and marking the best of their five responses. Students seldom mark their first response as their best, accenting to them that allowing more time to think often produces higher results.

Kingore, B. (2007). *Reaching All Learners.* Austin, TX: Professional Associates Publishing.

INDIVIDUAL RESPONSE BOARD

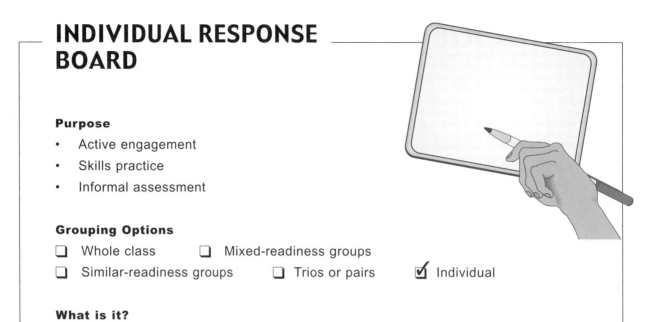

Purpose
- Active engagement
- Skills practice
- Informal assessment

Grouping Options

❑ Whole class   ❑ Mixed-readiness groups

❑ Similar-readiness groups   ❑ Trios or pairs   ☑ Individual

What is it?

Each student has a small board on which to record answers to questions posed by the teacher or examples prompted by the teacher.

Applications

Individual response boards are small chalkboards, wipe-off boards, or laminated four-by-six-inch index cards that students write on and hold up as appropriate to demonstrate their understanding. In response to the teacher's question, each student writes an answer and then holds up the response for the teacher and others to view. The strategy is best used with short-answer, often single word responses to account for differences in students' writing speeds.

The strategy is simple to use and encourages students to remain mentally engaged instead of mentally disconnecting as when only one student responds to a question. It provides a significant assessment device as teachers can instantly view students' understanding or misconceptions for a specific skill or concept. Teachers see which students quickly record the correct answer, who looks around for help before writing, and who needs reteaching or additional practice to reach understanding. Individual response boards can apply to many skills and content areas. Vary the tasks to include both words and images, thus appealing to different modes of learning. Figure 4.11 lists several application ideas to prompt thinking.

• **Figure 4.11** •
Individual Response Board:
Sample Activities

Spelling

* Write an *l*, draw two blanks, and then write a *k* (l--k). Now, figure out the word from this sentence and complete it on your board: I like to look through binoculars.
* Figure out which spelling word from our list that I am using in this sentence and write that word.

Math

* Write the answer each time I say a math fact.
* Draw the clock face to show this time.
* Write the formula for determining area.
* Draw this polygon.

Grammar

* As I point to a word in a sentence, write what part of speech it is.
* Add an appropriate adverb to this sentence: The squirrel ran up the tree trunk.

Science

* Write or draw one thing a magnet will attract.
* Write the name for each part of the plant as I point to it.
* Draw a water cycle.

Reading

* Sketch a picture of the cause that lead to this event.
* Write one trait of this character.
* What is the turning point in this story?

History

* Write the capital of each state as I point to it.
* As I read each statement, write whether it was most related to the Union or the Confederacy.

Health/drug awareness

* As I read each sentence, write whether it is a fact or opinion.

Kingore, B. (2007). *Reaching All Learners.* Austin, TX: Professional

INITIAL SENTENCES

Purpose

- Comprehension
- Analysis
- Mental engagement
- Grapheme-phoneme relationships
- Sequence
- Context clues
- Basic skill integration

Grouping Options

☐ Whole class ☐ Mixed-readiness groups

☐ Similar-readiness groups ☑ Trios or pairs ☑ Individual

What is it?

Initial sentences (Kingore, 2003) is a strategy that presents sentences for students to decipher in which only the first letter of each word is revealed. Students must analyze the initials in context to figure out the sentence.

Applications

Introduce the activity by writing on the board or overhead the initials of a simple, three-word sentence that students can easily interpret, such as *I i T* that means:

It is Tuesday.

ext, punctuation, and capitalization as clues to the
itional initial sentences until assured that students
model longer sentences that positively incorporate
ames to continue to captivate students' interest.

*Sarah and Jim
are leaders today.*

s. Austin, TX: Professional Associates Publishing.

DIRECTIONS

Using this strategy for directions is particularly advantageous to students with limited reading and writing skills. It commands students' attention. They are curious to figure out the statement and thus may attend to it more than just listening to or tuning out vocal commands. It activates high-level thinking and is more mentally engaging as it requires students to think and analyze rather than just listen.

Use the strategy with predictable direction statements that represent commands used repeatedly at specific times during the week, such as the following.

- *I i t f l.*   *It is time for lunch.*
- *P l u f m c.*   *Please line up for music class.*
- *G o y m m.*   *Get out your math manipulatives.*

The strategy has more flexible applications when the initial sentences are written on cards so they are quickly available in different locations. Write the initial sentences on the front of the card in clear, large print. Write the regular sentence on the back of the card as a reference.

STRETCH TIMES

After introducing the strategy, create engaging transitions or stretch breaks using initial sentences. First of all, complete the stretch time together using oral statements to provide students with experience in the process. Next, on the overhead or on separate cards, show the same directions as initial sentences revealing one at a time and waiting until the class has successfully followed each direction before revealing the next step. (Students look around and get clues from each other so everyone can do it.) Later, vary the sequence of the tasks and add different initial sentences to create additional stretch times.

Stretch Time

1. *S u.*   *Stand up.*
2. *S y a o y h.*   *Stretch your arms over your head.*
3. *T y t.*   *Touch your toes.*
4. *T y n.*   *Touch your nose.*
5. *T a 2 t.*   *Turn around two times.*
6. *S d a s.*   *Sit down and smile.*

Kingore, B. (2007). *Reaching All Learners.* Austin, TX: Professional Associates Publishing.

JIGSAW

Purpose
- Cooperative learning
- Multiple modalities
- Comprehension of nonfiction
- Summarization

Grouping Options

☐ Whole class   ☑ Mixed-readiness groups
☑ Similar-readiness groups   ☐ Trios or pairs   ☐ Individual

What is it?

Jigsaw is a cooperative strategy in which the teacher divides the text or a learning task into parts that individual students learn in order to teach to the rest of the group.

Applications

Like the pieces of a puzzle, teachers use the jigsaw strategy to divide written material about a topic into subtopics that create more manageable units for learning. Each member of a small group specializes in mastering a subpart and then teaches that part to the rest of the group so the parts combine to form a comprehensive whole. The intent is to effectively divide the task into meaningful and equally important segments so students learn complex material efficiently.

Initially, the teacher identifies the subtopics to introduce the process, but increased analysis and ownership occur when students assume the responsibility of determining the key subtopics within the main topic. Practice the strategy using short text selections before applying jigsaw to longer, complex text. Figure 4.12 outlines the sequence of the strategy.

Content Differentiation

To differentiate by content, the entire class can be involved in the strategy, but one or more advanced groups use different levels of material to respond at appropriate levels of complexity. To differentiate the content further, have groups investigate different topics when that adaptation better meets specific students' learning needs. Each group then teaches the rest of the class about the information they learned.

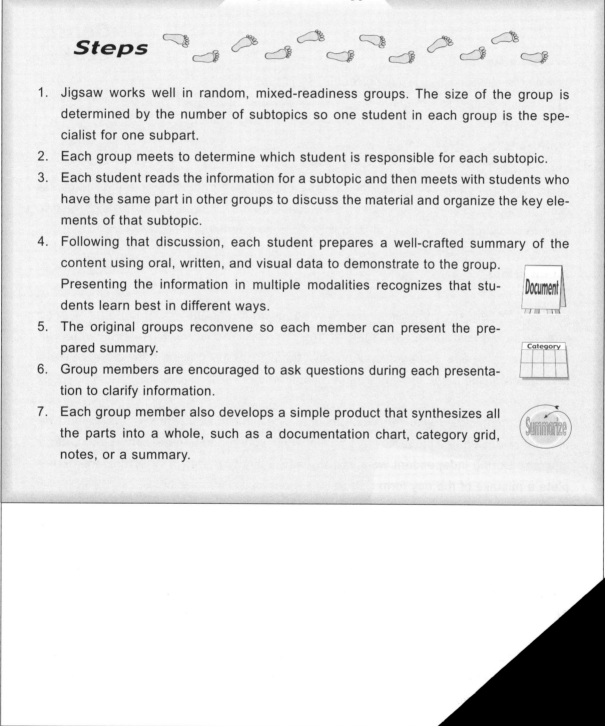

• Figure 4.12 •
Jigsaw Strategy

Steps

1. Jigsaw works well in random, mixed-readiness groups. The size of the group is determined by the number of subtopics so one student in each group is the specialist for one subpart.

2. Each group meets to determine which student is responsible for each subtopic.

3. Each student reads the information for a subtopic and then meets with students who have the same part in other groups to discuss the material and organize the key elements of that subtopic.

4. Following that discussion, each student prepares a well-crafted summary of the content using oral, written, and visual data to demonstrate to the group. Presenting the information in multiple modalities recognizes that students learn best in different ways.

5. The original groups reconvene so each member can present the prepared summary.

6. Group members are encouraged to ask questions during each presentation to clarify information.

7. Each group member also develops a simple product that synthesizes all the parts into a whole, such as a documentation chart, category grid, notes, or a summary.

Kingore, B. (2007). *Reaching All Learners.* Austin, TX: Professional

MISTAKE OF THE DAY

Oops! Mistake!

Purpose
- Skill applications
- Editing skills
- Analysis

Grouping Options
- ☐ Whole class
- ☐ Mixed-readiness groups
- ☐ Similar-readiness groups
- ☐ Trios or pairs
- ☑ Individual

What is it?

To apply targeted skills, one or more errors are purposely planted in the classroom for students to identify. Students are challenged to complete a mistake of the day form to explain how to correct all of the errors they can find.

Applications

A shoebox or other small box is wrapped with a brightly colored paper. The lid and the box are wrapped separately so the box can be opened. Mistake is written on each side of the box. For additional novelty, the word is misspelled many different ways and appears with a line drawn through it each time.

Communicate with the students that when the mistake box is displayed, the teacher or designated students have purposely included one or more errors in the day's lessons. Duri͏ work, as students identify the error or errors, they com- (Figure 4.13) and place it in the box.

e class discusses the error(s) and recognizes which to correct them. The discussion is lead by the teacher or the task. For additional mathematics applications, discussion by organizing and calculating the results. m of a graph or percentages.

sily adapted to any topic, concept, or skill of the it to call attention to a frequently occurring error useful strategy to call attention to errors present

rs. Austin, TX: Professional Associates Publishing.

in students' written mechanics, scientific understanding, historical knowledge, or math applications. Basic skills and thinking levels from simple to more complex can be applied.

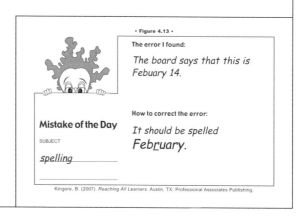

• Figure 4.13 •

The error I found:

The board says that this is Febuary 14.

How to correct the error:

It should be spelled February.

Mistake of the Day

SUBJECT

spelling

Kingore, B. (2007). *Reaching All Learners.* Austin, TX: Professional Associates Publishing.

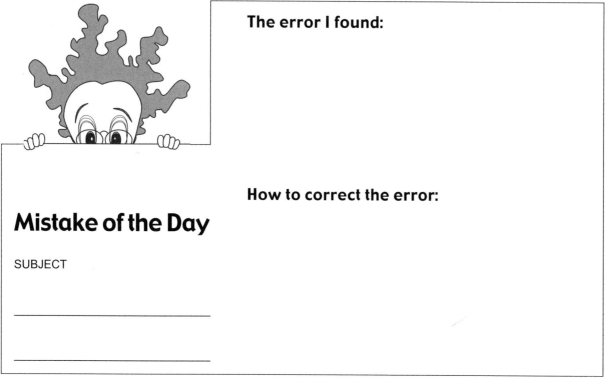

• **Figure 4.13** •

The error I found:

How to correct the error:

Mistake of the Day

SUBJECT

Kingore, B. (2007). *Reaching All Learners.* Austin, TX: Professional Associates Publishing.

NOMINATE

Purpose
- Recognition of individual work
- Idea sharing among students
- Self-esteem
- Closure

Grouping Options
- ☑ Whole class
- ☐ Similar-readiness groups
- ☐ Mixed-readiness groups
- ☐ Trios or pairs
- ☐ Individual

What is it?

Instead of asking individuals to volunteer to share their work with the class, teachers invite the class to nominate which students should share their high-quality responses.

Applications

Teachers like a few examples to be shared with the whole class after small group work is completed. Typically, when the teacher asks who wants to share, the same verbal students volunteer. Nominate is a strategy that results in a wider pool of students being considered.

After pair-sharing or small group work, nominate is a strategy to use as an alternative to the standard question: *Who would like to share their work with the class?* Invite class members to nominate someone whose work they saw or heard that they think everyone should share. Usually several students speak up and say: *I nominate _____.* When a student is nominated, that student is empowered and can either share or pass. In this way, a student is recognized by peers but is not forced to share in front of the whole class. The quiet, introspective student can be nominated and thus receive the self-esteem boost of having the quality of work noted.

Most students elect to share when they are nominated and enjoy that someone recognizes their work. A few students may pass just to test their power to do so. Even when they pass, however, they still have the satisfaction of being recognized as doing worthy work.

Kingore, B. (2007). *Reaching All Learners.* Austin, TX: Professional Associates Publishing.

NOTE TAKING

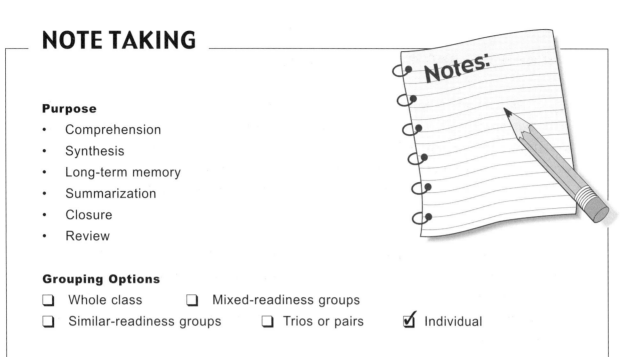

Purpose

- Comprehension
- Synthesis
- Long-term memory
- Summarization
- Closure
- Review

Grouping Options

- ☐ Whole class   ☐ Mixed-readiness groups
- ☐ Similar-readiness groups   ☐ Trios or pairs   ☑ Individual

What is it?

Note taking is directly related to summarization and is a key achievement strategy that requires students to synthesize information (Marzano, 2001). It helps the brain chuck information for long-term memory. To take effective notes, a student must determine the most important information and record that information in a succinct manner.

Applications

Note taking provides students with a tool for identifying and organizing the most important aspects of the information they are learning. Instead of a skill to teach students to respond to lectures, note taking is now viewed as a strategy that increases students' active engagement in learning, helps them process information, and guides their memory.

- As a closure task, provide a few minutes at the end of a discussion for students to revisit their notes. This process enables students to revise misconceptions or develop clearer ways to synthesize the information.

- Encourage students to use their notes when working with their study buddy to compare perceptions and review information.

Visual techniques and templates guide students in their note taking. The four techniques shared here also serve as visual proof of the student's preparation.

Kingore, B. (2007). *Reaching All Learners.* Austin, TX: Professional Associates Publishing.

STICKY NOTES AND HIGHLIGHTING TAPE

As students read, they place sticky notes or highlighting tape in the text to mark significant information. For example, when sequence is a target skill, children use sticky notes to flag and number the key events in the story. At other times, they write questions and personal connections that occur to them as they read fiction and nonfiction. Teachers provide the size of sticky notes that best matches the children's need for writing space.

Students enjoy using sticky-notes as they require minimum extra time and help students remember ideas. Sticky notes and highlighting tape do not harm surfaces and are easily moved to reorganize or expand thoughts into complete sentences or paragraphs. This simple technique is equally appropriate for special needs students, young children, and older students.

CONCEPT MAPS OR WEBS

Concept maps work well for note taking, particularly when the graphic uses different sizes of shapes to indicate the importance of ideas and uses lines to establish sequence and relationships. The rectangle example here shows that hierarchy of importance and relationships. A potential disadvantage of using concept maps for note taking, however, is the limited space provided for information and the preset number of relationships dictated by the template.

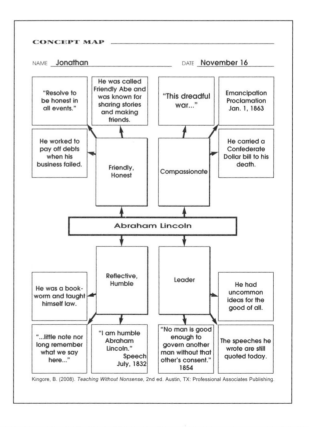

THE CORNELL NOTE TAKING SYSTEM

The Cornell Note Taking System, as illustrated on the next page, uses three sections to organize information and is more appropriate for upper elementary and middle school students. Intended as a lecture response, it is equally valid for students to use as they read complex material. First, students use the column on the right to record the information as meaningfully as possible. Secondly, they review that information to reduce the ideas and facts to concise jottings in the left column. Finally, they summarize the notes at the bottom of each page.

NOTES & SYMBOLS TEMPLATE

A simplified variation of the Cornell system offers the advantage

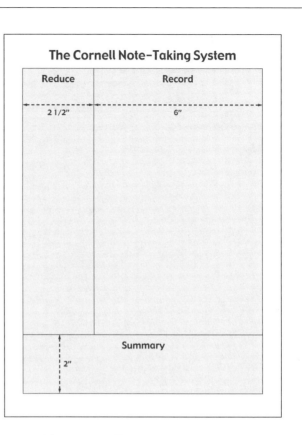

of incorporating multiple modes of learning to aid memory (Figure 4.14). While all students are encouraged to respond to all three sections on the template, most students have stronger responses on either the right or the left side, corresponding to their learning strengths. The information recording proceeds from left to right and top to bottom to parallel the directionality taught with literacy skills.

The left column focuses upon words and phrases to relate the key ideas; the right column accents visual symbolic connections to that same information. Students then use their words and symbols to process the information into a summary to write in the bottom section.

Kingore, B. (2007). *Reaching All Learners.* Austin, TX: Professional Associates Publishing.

• **Figure 4.14** •

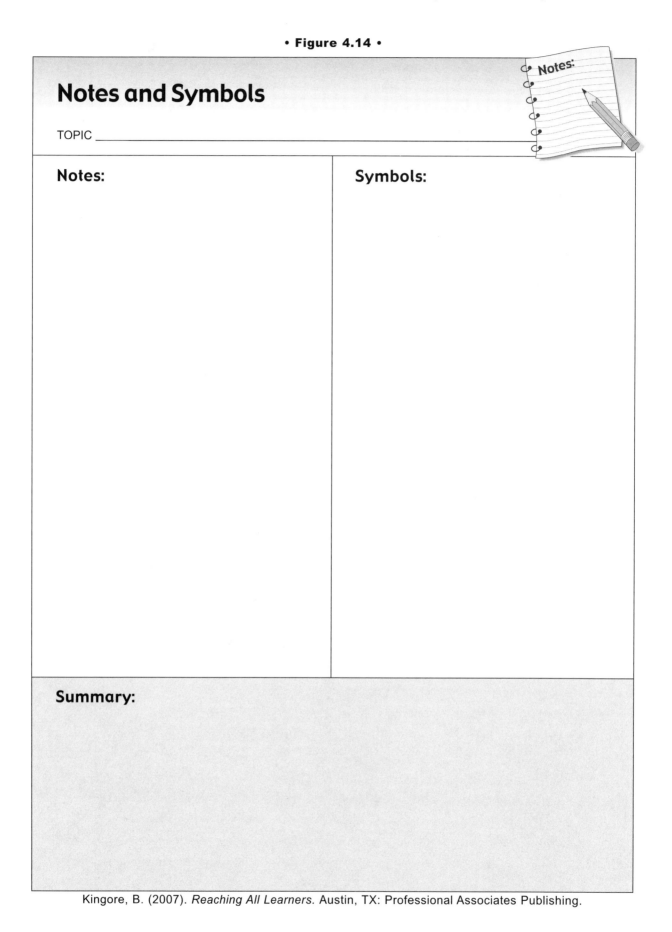

Notes and Symbols

TOPIC _____

Notes:	Symbols:

Summary:

Kingore, B. (2007). *Reaching All Learners.* Austin, TX: Professional Associates Publishing.

PAPER WAD REVIEW

Purpose

- Review
- Practicing basic skills
- Student interaction
- Bodily-kinesthetic task

Grouping Options

☑ Whole class ☑ Mixed-readiness groups

❑ Similar-readiness groups ❑ Trios or pairs ❑ Individual

What is it?

The teacher writes multiple concepts and skills on separate strips of paper, wads each strip, mixes them up, and challenges students to cooperatively rematch the parts.

Applications

A paper wad review is a lively strategy choice for practicing basic skills and reviewing content. Its novelty increases students' interest and attention as it invites students to move and interact. It works very well as a small group task, yet it can be used to involve the whole class in a review of skills and content.

Cut apart a paper containing skill applications or topic-related questions and answers so that each piece contains part of the information. Each piece is then crumbled into a paper wad. Mix up the wads before each student chooses one and tries to complete a match by finding the student who has the missing part. Math facts, coin-values, uppercase-lowercase letters, phonics, synonyms-antonyms, and affix-root matches are examples of skill applications. Concept examples include cause-effect, matching key terms to a cloze sentence, and matching a question with an answer. When mastery of skills is a goal, the same paper wads can be reused as frequently as needed or as long as student interest remains high.

As a variation for kinesthetic learners, students select a paper wad to toss at one another, catch, and match. This variation works well outside or when students have experience with paper wad review and can have fun with the process without losing self-control.

Kingore, B. (2007). *Reaching All Learners.* Austin, TX: Professional Associates Publishing.

SHARE TRIOS

Purpose

- Peer interaction and feedback
- Process analysis
- Oral presentation skills
- Self-assessment

Grouping Options

☐ Whole class   ☐ Mixed-readiness groups
☐ Similar-readiness groups   ☑ Trios or pairs   ☐ Individual

What is it?

A peer-share trio is a fast-paced strategy for students to share and compare their work. In groups of three, each student shares and discusses a product that is in process or completed. Typically, each student decides which product to share with two peers. In approximately ten minutes of class time, each student's work is featured and each student profits from learning about the work of two peers.

Applications

The groups can be formed randomly or by student choice, depending upon the teacher's objectives. A trio is a perfect size for an efficient use of class time while students model different ideas to one another. A result of peer-share trios is that students discover it is rewarding to share products, discuss new ideas with others, and elicit others' perceptions about products.

To introduce the strategy, each student selects a completed product and plans two things to say about it. To prepare as listeners, each student plans one question to ask that is not evaluative and focuses on the process or the interest of the presenter. Organize students into trios and announce which student presents first: *The person wearing the most red is first to present a product.* As the trios present, the teacher circulates among the groups writing notes to informally assess and guide future instruction. After the peer-share trios finish, debrief as a class to complement what went well, ask students what they enjoyed, and brainstorm refinements that would make the process better next time. Later, students select products in process and use the trio format to elicit ideas for revisions.

Kingore, B. (2007). *Reaching All Learners.* Austin, TX: Professional Associates Publishing.

A simple way to prompt peer interactions during peer sharing with young children is to post and accent investigative words. Prompts, such as *why, how, where,* and *what,* encourage more open-ended responses and less yes-or-no answers. Another way is to discuss and possibly post questions intended to focus on the process and the product rather than evaluating the person. Figure 4.15 provides several examples.

A peer-share trio is an effective strategy to help students increase their comfort when orally presenting information to an audience. Students comment that they feel more confident presenting to a small group than to the whole class. It is a prequel to productive peer revision workshops and student-involved conferences as it promotes self-assessment of process and product. When appropriate, designate a particular product assignment for all students to share and compare different versions and results.

• Figure 4.15 •
Questions for Peer-Share Trios

Question	Purpose
What do you like about this work?	Focusing on positive feelings helps students recognize those aspects of their work.
What gave you the idea?	Discussing idea sources may give others new directions.
What did you want to accomplish with this work?	It is important for students to understand that each product or project should have a personal purpose and to help students evaluate whether or not that purpose was realized.
What did you do to plan it?	Discussing organization and management techniques models ideas to other students regarding how to plan their work.
Is there anything about your work you would like to change?	This question is not intended to make students feel dissatisfied with what they have done but rather to accent the idea that it is healthy to consider improvements or changes.
Have you done anything else like it?	Great products often result from a chain of accomplishments where one work influences the next.
What else would you like to know about this topic?	One purpose of school is to entice students with the idea that there are always more interesting and often exciting things to learn.
What do you want to work on next?	Establishing and sharing future goals increases the intrinsic motivation and goal setting of some students.

Kingore, B. (2007). *Reaching All Learners.* Austin, TX: Professional Associates Publishing.

PICTURE 1000 WORDS

Purpose

- High-level thinking
- Comprehension
- Basic skill practice
- Visual-spatial learning
- Vocabulary
- Content connections
- Informal assessment

Grouping Options

☑ Whole class   ☑ Mixed-readiness groups
☐ Similar-readiness groups   ☐ Trios or pairs   ☑ Individual

What is it?

Use interesting, topic-related pictures and complexly-detailed illustrations from children's literature selections to promote high-level thinking and basic skill integration.

Applications

As the adage goes, a picture is worth 1000 words. Pictures are readily accessible and provide a visual prompt to engage students in practicing and extending skills as they study an interesting picture.

- Name all of the colors.
- List and categorize items in the picture by parts of speech.
- Find an item that begins with _____.
- How many rhymes can you create for items in the picture?
- Find an item with three-syllables in its name.
- Use more than one language to identify multiple items in the scene.
- Are there more _____ or _____ in the picture?
- Arrange these five pictures as a continuum and explain your reasoning.
- You are something in the picture. Describe yourself to us so we can figure you out.
- Orally describe the picture.
- How many adjectives can you list to describe the picture?
- Make up a math story problem that goes with this picture.

Kingore, B. (2007). *Reaching All Learners.* Austin, TX: Professional Associates Publishing.

Pictures effectively help students generate ideas for writing or story development. Visual learners benefit substantially when an image accompanies a writing prompt.

• Write about the picture from an unexpected point of view.

• Explain a connection you make to the picture.

• Develop multiple analogies.

> *This picture is like _____ because _____.*
>
> *The _____ in this picture is like _____ because _____.*

• Since a picture is worth 1000 words, find a picture about a topic you are interested in researching and write a 1000-word composition relating your research about that topic. Incorporate numerous pictures and symbols in your response.

Pictures are a useful tool when assessing students' comprehension in any content area. Use a picture to elicit what students know and understand.

• Identify specific items or people in the picture, such as science equipment or the names of early explorers.

• Describe the scene and elaborate causes and effects related to that picture.

• Relate what happened before or after the picture according to your reading.

• Analyze from whose perspective the picture is depicted.

Kingore, B. (2007). *Reaching All Learners.* Austin, TX: Professional Associates Publishing.

PLANNING SHEET _____

Purpose

* Analyzing
* Planning and organizing before acting
* Mental engagement
* Preassessment

Grouping Options

❑ Whole class   ❑ Mixed-readiness groups
❑ Similar-readiness groups   ❑ Trios or pairs   ☑ Individual

What is it?

Ask students to think for a moment and plan a response by writing or sketching. Simple advance planning can dramatically increase the depth and originality of their work.

Applications

When idea generation is important, ask students to use scrap paper or an individual response board as a planning sheet. Students use words and images to quickly record ideas and plan their procedures or responses. The emphasis is on the planning and quality of ideas; spelling and handwriting are not critical features at this time. This sloppy-copy approach encourages more students to think freely and organize their ideas before speaking. Try saying to them: *Write which _____ you think is most important before we share ideas;* or *Write your best response to the question before we compare.*

During class discussions, a simple planning sheet encourages students to think and record information rather than just shout it out or raise their hands eagerly before they have a solid idea. Planning sheets help students form productive habits: *We think and plan before we speak or write.* Students produce more ideas and are more actively engaged when they develop a concrete plan rather than just think about the topic.

* Planning sheets integrate well with the think-pair-share strategy used in cooperative learning. The teacher poses a prompt for individual students to think about and quickly record ideas on a planning sheet. Then, each student pairs with another student to compare ideas before coming back together as a whole class or group to share.

* Students use planning sheets to organize products before they begin the task. As they plan, circulate among the students to coach, facilitate, and preassess needs.

Kingore, B. (2007). *Reaching All Learners.* Austin, TX: Professional Associates Publishing.

PROCESS LETTER

Purpose

- Assessment
- Metacognition
- Sequence
- Analysis
- Synthesis

Grouping Options

☐ Whole class ☐ Mixed-readiness groups
☐ Similar-readiness groups ☐ Trios or pairs ☑ Individual

What is it?

A process letter is an informal but illuminating assessment device. After learning a process, students write a letter explaining how to complete that process.

Applications

When teachers have taught a process in any content area, they want to ensure that students understand and can incorporate the process as their own. Having students write a process letter is a simple, open-ended way to assess the depth of their understanding.

A process letter is a think aloud in a letter format. The format adds novelty to the expository writing and is usually brief enough that students can complete it in about twenty minutes. Students write to a real or fictitious person of their choice. Many students have fun with this selection and incorporate clever, often humorous connections to the person they are addressing in their letter. The strategy requires students to metacognitively dissect the process and then synthesize it into a letter format that also integrates many conventions of writing, particularly paragraphs, punctuation, and capitalization skills.

Evaluating process letters saves instructional time.

Evaluating process letters involves more time than using an answer key, but can be reasonably managed with a well-crafted rubric. Furthermore, teachers find the process more interesting and diagnostically beneficial than simple

Kingore, B. (2007). *Reaching All Learners.* Austin, TX: Professional Associates Publishing.

correct answers. When reading a process letter, the teacher is assured which students understand, and when a misconception or inaccurate information is evident, the teacher knows exactly which part to reteach rather than start over teaching the entire process again. Evaluating process letters saves instructional time.

SCIENCE PROCESS LETTER

Students write a letter explaining how to conduct a science experiment or use specific science equipment. Writing a clear and accurate process explanation increases students' and the teacher's confidence that students are able to safely and independently proceed with the process.

MATH PROCESS LETTER

Students write a letter delineating how to complete a math problem that represents the skills and concepts currently being studied. Motivate high-quality responses from students by explaining that writing a complete and accurate process explanation challenges them to demonstrate mastery of the math process instead of completing additional practice sheets of math problems.

Dear Dr. Einstein,

I am writing to tell you about the life cycle of a frog. There are five stages I will tell you.

First, frogs lay eggs in water or a wet place. Second, the egg cell splits. It grows into an embryo that hatches into a tadpole. Third, the tadpole gets bigger and grows hind legs. Fourth, the tadpole grows four legs, the tail gets smaller, and lungs develop. Fifth, the tadpole develops into a frog. When the frog lays eggs, the cycle begins all over again.

Cycles go on and on. That is like your work. Your work goes on and on to help us understand science. I want to be a scientist, too.

Sincerely,
Erika Jameson

QUICK SKETCH

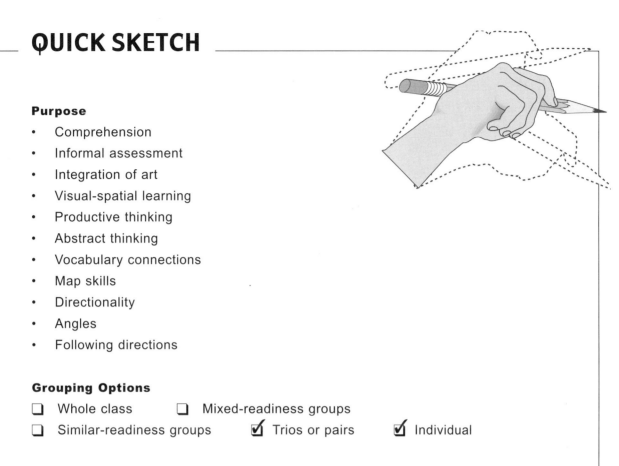

Purpose
*   Comprehension
*   Informal assessment
*   Integration of art
*   Visual-spatial learning
*   Productive thinking
*   Abstract thinking
*   Vocabulary connections
*   Map skills
*   Directionality
*   Angles
*   Following directions

Grouping Options
☐ Whole class   ☐ Mixed-readiness groups
☐ Similar-readiness groups   ☑ Trios or pairs   ☑ Individual

What is it?

The quick sketch strategy activates right-brain responses to content by asking students to graphically represent information.

Applications

At an appropriate juncture during a teacher-directed lesson, the teacher pauses and asks students to quickly complete a sketch to illustrate a concept or point. The term quick sketch is used to free students from worrying about the quality of their art talent. The intent is active engagement and personal interpretation of content rather than finely developed illustrations. Research documents that art responses provide students additional contexts to augment memory and comprehension—particularly regarding specific subject vocabulary (ASCD, 2006).

Many students and adults have convinced themselves that they cannot draw well. A simple sketch technique taught in art courses is useful to build confidence in one's ability to draw and graphically represent ideas. Model with students to begin repeatedly drawing overlapping spirals without lifting the pencil from the paper. Draw

Kingore, B. (2007). *Reaching All Learners.* Austin, TX: Professional Associates Publishing.

the spirals continuously, making them larger, then smaller, and moving them in different directions. Continue sketching until the desired image is generally filled in and the object being drawn is complete.

Tell students to move their spirals to draw a simple shape, such as a horse. Incorporate simple map, directionality, and math skills by asking students to continue spiraling left, up, east, or at a 90-degree angle. Most students are surprised and satisfied with their results and now have a technique that frees them to complete quick sketches for content applications.

Vocabulary

- Students sketch images to picture a content-specific word or context that illustrates their comprehension.
- Working in pairs, one student begins a quick sketch of a content-specific word while the other student watches and tries to identify the picture, state the vocabulary word, and spell it before the sketch is complete.

Written composition

- Highly visual and spatial students benefit from sketching ideas and sequences before trying to encode their ideas in words.
- Quick sketch allows students who are not comfortable with their drawing skills to include illustrations with their written compositions.

Math

- Students illustrate a math problem or solution.
- Math story problems can include a quick sketch illustrating the key elements of the problem.

Kingore, B. (2007). *Reaching All Learners.* Austin, TX: Professional Associates Publishing.

REBUS

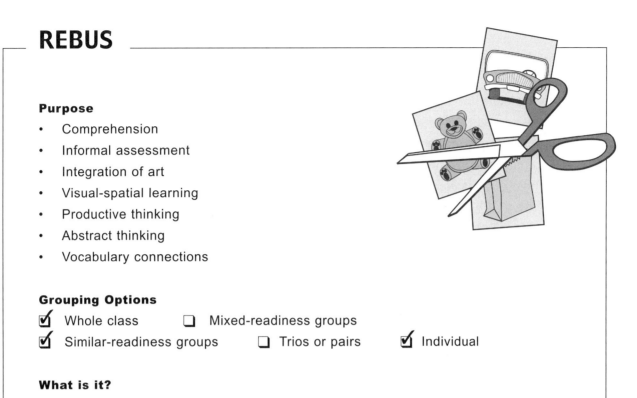

Purpose

- Comprehension
- Informal assessment
- Integration of art
- Visual-spatial learning
- Productive thinking
- Abstract thinking
- Vocabulary connections

Grouping Options

☑ Whole class   ☐ Mixed-readiness groups

☑ Similar-readiness groups   ☐ Trios or pairs   ☑ Individual

What is it?

Rebus is a strategy to support young or struggling readers and writers. In text, simple pictures are substituted for words, or a picture is provided with a word, to enhance comprehension with a less-demanding reading level.

Applications

Rebus is a visually appealing strategy that enables young or struggling readers to comprehend written text. Incorporating both a word and an illustration provides more contexts for these students to support their reading development.

Rebus pictures are typically simple, literal representations. Pictures of common items, living things, and daily needs, such as washing hands, are available in clip-art books and on many software programs. Teachers of young, ELL, or special needs students incorporate these pictures in written directions to enable students to experience greater independence when reading and following directions.

 Please come to the door.    *Cut out five pictures. Paste them.*

Kingore, B. (2007). *Reaching All Learners.* Austin, TX: Professional Associates Publishing.

For phonics instruction, teachers provide copies of pictures with a targeted phonics skill, such as pictures that begin with the same phoneme. Students cut around several pictures and use one or more of them in sentences they write. When additional support is needed, teachers begin by displaying patterns for sentences planned so multiple pictures can be inserted to complete the meaning. Later, students develop their own rebus sentences without a pattern.

* *The _____ is big.*
* *I see a _____ and a _____.*

Students use rebus writing to retell fiction or nonfiction, to write the sequence of steps in a science experiment, or to convey information gained through their research. The pictures can be provided, students can draw their own pictures, or combinations of both can be used as students complete rebus responses.

Visual-spatial learners with more sophisticated literacy skills also enjoy rebus. They can use more abstract illustrations as symbols to incorporate into fiction and nonfiction writing.

Kingore, B. (2007). *Reaching All Learners.* Austin, TX: Professional Associates Publishing.

RESPONSE ROUNDS

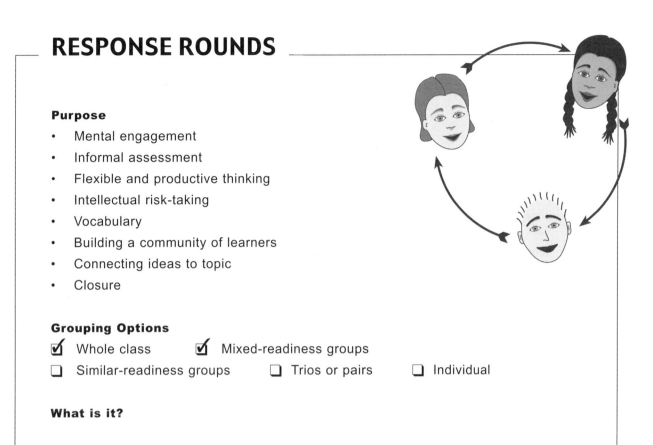

Purpose
- Mental engagement
- Informal assessment
- Flexible and productive thinking
- Intellectual risk-taking
- Vocabulary
- Building a community of learners
- Connecting ideas to topic
- Closure

Grouping Options
- ☑ Whole class
- ☑ Mixed-readiness groups
- ☐ Similar-readiness groups
- ☐ Trios or pairs
- ☐ Individual

What is it?

A teacher uses the response rounds strategy to elicit responses to the topic or examples of a concept or skill from multiple students. The teacher states a problem, situation, or category and asks students to take turns responding with an example. The goal is to elicit a response from every student as often as possible.

Applications

At an appropriate juncture during a teacher-directed lesson, the teacher pauses and asks students to respond with examples or personal connections to the topic or concept. For example, a teacher states a sentence stem and asks children to complete it in as many different but content appropriate ways as possible.
- The best book we've read is _____.
- My favorite is _____.
- I use this skill when _____.
- An example is _____.
- One thing I'll remember is _____.
- I would like to change _____.
- I expected _____.
- One thing I learned _____.
- I wish _____.

Kingore, B. (2007). *Reaching All Learners.* Austin, TX: Professional Associates Publishing.

The strategy is more engaging when a fast pace is encouraged. The responses progress quickly from student to student around the room, often continuing until all students respond.

To promote diverse responses and greater depth to students' thinking, elevate students' attention by stipulating that the same response may not be used more than once. This variation encourages students to actively listen to each other and consider multiple aspects and attributes of the topic.

The strategy applies to multiple topics and models that multiple ideas and intellectual risk-taking are valued. A response round is particularly applicable as a closure task. After students have been involved in a range of different learning tasks, they come back together as a community of learners and individually share with the whole class by responding to the prompt: *One thing I accomplished today* _____; or *Today I worked on* _____.

Addressing Potential Problems

At times, a student may be unable to think of a response. Allow that student to temporarily pass by saying: *Pass now and signal me when to come back to you for your response.* That reaction lightens the immediate pressure on the student but extends the expectation that the student should continue to think of possible responses. At the conclusion of the response round, if the student has not signaled a readiness to respond, return to that student. If the student still does not have an idea to share, consider a reaction such as: *We appreciate that you kept thinking and listening. Sometimes thinking takes longer for all of us.*

If any student seems consistently frazzled by the strategy, consider meeting with that student privately to provide an advance notice of the next response round topic. Arrange with that student that you will begin the round with her first so she can predict and feel more in control.

Kingore, B. (2007). *Reaching All Learners.* Austin, TX: Professional Associates Publishing.

RIDDLES

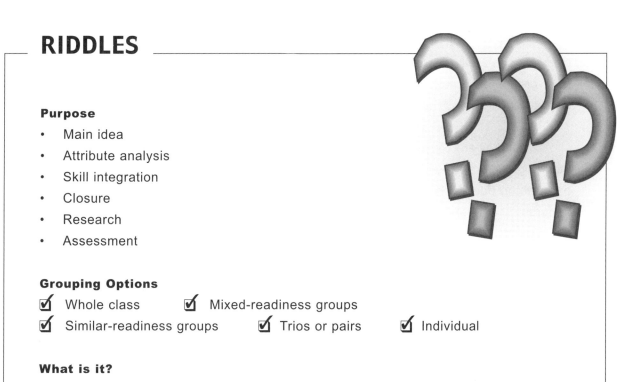

Purpose

• Main idea

• Attribute analysis

• Skill integration

• Closure

• Research

• Assessment

Grouping Options

☑ Whole class   ☑ Mixed-readiness groups

☑ Similar-readiness groups   ☑ Trios or pairs   ☑ Individual

What is it?

Riddles present a puzzling question, problem, or series of statements that other students must decipher. They require high-level thinking to produce and to solve. Using riddles with content requires students to think and demonstrate their understanding of the content.

Applications

Riddles pique students' curiosity and provide an interesting format for sharing information and integrating skills.

 I am a spelling word.
I have more letters than most of the words, but I only have two syllables.
Which word am I?

 I am a prime number that is less than the square r
I have two digits.
What am I?

Most riddles are composed of an organized series of a concept that lead students to conclude the main idea. The g results when students work to analyze content, prioritize att are the most significant, and then develop a riddle to share

Kingore, B. (2007). *Reaching All Learners.* Austin, TX: Profes

closure task, orally share several riddles about the content with the group. Then, ask pairs or trios of students to proceed independently at their desks to create topic-related riddles for other students to complete.

Riddles are a child-appealing format for relating similarities and differences--the most significant strategy for increasing student achievement (Marzano, 2001). The parts of the riddle can include examples and non-examples that challenge students to understand and analyze content.

 I am an oviparous animal.
I have four legs, a tail, and a long tongue.
I am not a fowl or a mammal.
Which animal am I?

Riddles can be oral or written and prove effective with all age groups. Since students enjoy both deciphering and creating riddles, they remain more mentally engaged in the task.

(2007). *Reaching All Learners.* Austin, TX: Professional Associates Publishing.

ROLL CALL LEARNING

Purpose
- Integrating basic skills and content
- Mental engagement
- Recognizing individuals
- Informal assessment
- Closure

Grouping Options
☐ Whole class ☐ Mixed-readiness groups
☐ Similar-readiness groups ☐ Trios or pairs ☑ Individual

What is it?

The teacher calls a student's name and asks for responses relating to the current topic. This instantly-ready strategy integrates well with any topic or grade level.

Applications

Learning psychology suggests that a person's first name is important to recognize and show respect for individuals. Yet, researchers note that some teachers use collective nouns most of the day when addressing the students. *Boys and girls, class,* and *kids* are often used as attention commands. Roll call learning is a simple strategy that positively accents the names of children. Say to the class: *When I call your name, answer with* (inject a category or skill related to the current topic of study). When appropriate, encourage students to listen to each other and think of a different response each time. Multiple concepts and skills, such as the following are easily integrated with this strategy.

- One attribute of _____
- A carnivore
- A shape with more than three sides
- One way to solve _____

- A synonym for _____
- Something that _____
- A prime number
- A three-syllable word

This strategy is a useful way to mentally engage children and integrate basic skills as the children get in line, transition between learning tasks, and wait for others to finish. It is an instantly available strategy that is also effective at transition times or when a change of pace is needed during a lesson. It is useful as a closure activity that demands little time but allows each student to demonstrate understanding.

Kingore, B. (2007). *Reaching All Learners.* Austin, TX: Professional Associates Publishing.

SCAMPER

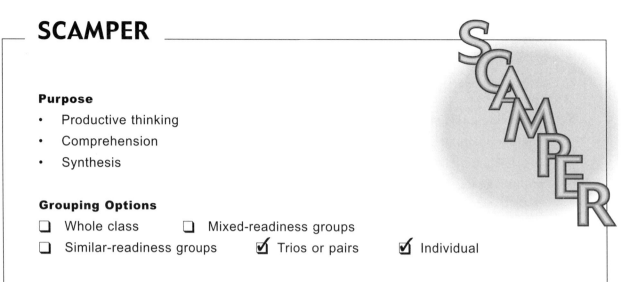

Purpose

- Productive thinking
- Comprehension
- Synthesis

Grouping Options

- ☐ Whole class   ☐ Mixed-readiness groups
- ☐ Similar-readiness groups   ☑ Trios or pairs   ☑ Individual

What is it?

SCAMPER is an acronym that represents verbs to prompt productive thinking. After modeling, many students can use the strategy independently to promote revisions and new ideas.

Applications

SCAMPER, defined by Eberle (1996) from an initial list by Alex Osborn, was previously discussed as a teacher tool for differentiating a lesson. However, students can use SCAMPER as a revision tool or to prompt ideas during problem solving or research.

Since students are frequently reluctant to revise their work, a productive thinking tool is an asset and a motivator. Students mentally skim through the elements of SCAMPER to guide revisions. If an event or paragraph isn't effective, students question themselves about which words or ideas can be substituted, combined, modified, or eliminated, such as considering ways to rearrange the sequence of the plot to better involve the reader.

SCAMPER is also an effective strategy for students to use to prompt original ideas during problem-solving opportunities and to focus original research investigations. Students can SCAMPER ideas to incorporate higher thinking levels and evolve from excessive fact listing to analyzing, evaluating, and creating. Challenge students to determine if they are producing high-level ideas by plotting the updated Bloom's (Anderson & Krathwohl, 2001) level of thinking for each idea. Using Figure 4.16, students then rank their ideas to determine the best ones to incorporate.

Kingore, B. (2007). *Reaching All Learners.* Austin, TX: Professional Associates Publishing.

• Figure 4.16 •

Bloom's Taxonomy Updated							
Create							
Evaluate							
Analyze							
Apply							
Understand							
Remember							

SCAMPER

TOPIC _____

Ranking	Substitute	Combine	Adapt	Modify, minify, magnify	Put to other use	Eliminate	Rearrange, reverse

SCAMPER Adapted from Eberle (1996). Bloom's Taxonomy Updated by Anderson & Krathwohl (2001).

Kingore, B. (2007). *Reaching All Learners.* Austin, TX: Professional Associates Publishing.

SIGN-UPS

Purpose
- Flexible grouping
- Student choice
- Reteaching

Grouping Options
- ☐ Whole class
- ☑ Similar-readiness groups
- ☑ Individual
- ☑ Mixed-readiness groups
- ☑ Trios or pairs

What is it?

The sign-ups strategy is a more unique and student-responsible means of forming small groups for reteaching, skill practice, and extensions. The teacher organizes the opportunity for a variety of small group sessions, and students self-nominate to participate.

Applications

Sign-up is a strategy that invites students to take responsibility for learning. Groups are organized by students' self-nominating their participation in specific focus groups. The teacher designates a variety of options and provides sign-up sheets listing each specific session. Sign-ups are used to form interest groups, projects, and skills groups. Frequently, silent reading time is included as one option.

> **With the pressures of learning standards, teachers discover that sign-ups is a fruitful and less stigmatizing strategy for reteaching or refining skills.**

All students must sign-up for one of the options. Students write their name on the list that they feel would be most beneficial to them. (Teachers can also privately and tactfully suggest that specific students sign-up for needed sessions.)

With the pressures of learning standards, teachers discover that sign-ups is a fruitful and less stigmatizing strategy for reteaching or refining skills. Students are often aware of their needs and know when they would benefit from a skill group's focus. Students sign-up for the sessions that most interest them or for the skill sessions they believe they most need for practice or clarification. During skills sessions, they meet

Kingore, B. (2007). *Reaching All Learners.* Austin, TX: Professional Associates Publishing.

with the teacher for reteaching or clarification. Other students work in background groups on sustained silent reading or extension tasks to develop depth and complexity. Students who have acquired grade-level skills sometimes elect to sign-up for a skills group just for refinement or reinforcement.

Sign-ups is a simple way to differentiate instruction by content and process. The element of choice is a powerful means to increase student ownership in learning. The resulting group sessions can be brief and easily repeated as needed.

Variation

Post the sign-up notice but provide cards for students to write on to sign-up for the group. Cards promote a more personal rather than public view. More students elect to sign-up by their personal need when not influenced by what others select on the list of options. Use small index cards as an easy way to sort the names for grouping.

Kingore, B. (2007). *Reaching All Learners.* Austin, TX: Professional Associates Publishing.

SUMMARIZATION

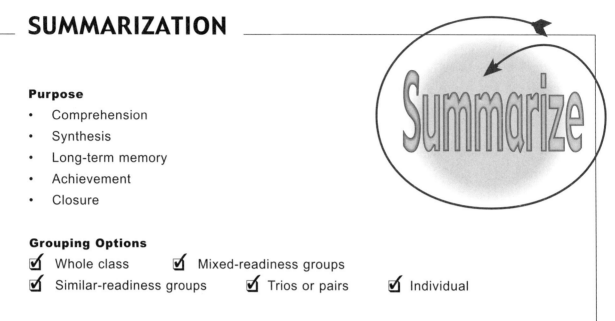

Purpose

- Comprehension
- Synthesis
- Long-term memory
- Achievement
- Closure

Grouping Options

☑ Whole class   ☑ Mixed-readiness groups

☑ Similar-readiness groups   ☑ Trios or pairs   ☑ Individual

What is it?

Summarization is a key achievement strategy that requires students to synthesize information. It is one of the most significant strategies for increasing students' achievement (Marzano, 2001). It aids the brain's chunking of concepts by requiring students to determine the essence of the text in a succinct manner.

Applications

Since summarization is so directly related to long-term memory and achievement, it is a strategy teachers must strive to apply to most lessons. Teachers learn to stop a lesson in time to summarize as a closure because it is more important that students remember the concept than that the teacher finishes covering the lesson. Wormeli (2005) asserts that we should teach students that summarizing makes the content stick in their minds.

Summarization requires that students understand and are able to analyze material at a complex level. It is more involved than many people assume, as it requires multiple high-level thinking skills as outlined in the sequence in Figure 4.17.

The proper length of a summary is a concern for some students. Two characters in Konigsburg's *Silent to the Bone* (2000) express experiences with a technique that they refer to as SIAS or summary in a sentence. A summary for a paragraph may indeed be one sentence—specifically a topic sentence or main idea. With longer discourse, however, a summary is composed of a main idea and key information from the beginning, middle, and end of the text connected with transition words. Wormeli (2005) recommends that a summary should only be ten to twenty-five percent of brief text and one percent of lengthy text, such as a novel.

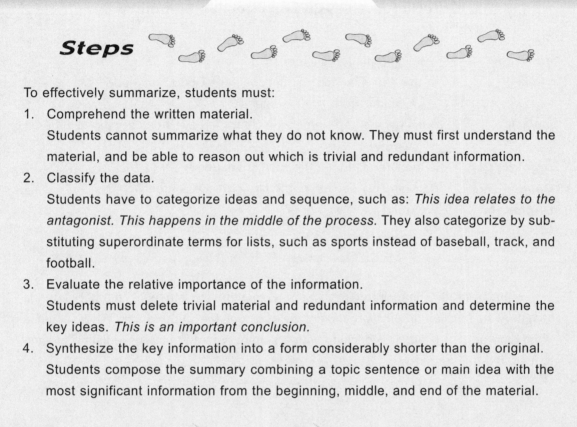

• **Figure 4.17** •
Summarization

Steps

To effectively summarize, students must:

1. Comprehend the written material.

   Students cannot summarize what they do not know. They must first understand the material, and be able to reason out which is trivial and redundant information.

2. Classify the data.

   Students have to categorize ideas and sequence, such as: *This idea relates to the antagonist. This happens in the middle of the process.* They also categorize by substituting superordinate terms for lists, such as sports instead of baseball, track, and football.

3. Evaluate the relative importance of the information.

   Students must delete trivial material and redundant information and determine the key ideas. *This is an important conclusion.*

4. Synthesize the key information into a form considerably shorter than the original.

   Students compose the summary combining a topic sentence or main idea with the most significant information from the beginning, middle, and end of the material.

CATEGORIZE ➤ *DELETE* ➤ *COMPOSE*

Transition words are vital for writing well-crafted summaries as they enable students to smoothly segue from one idea to the next. As a class, develop a list of transition words as visual prompts that students add to and incorporate into their summaries.

• Additionally	• Finally	• However
• After	• For example	• Next
• Also	• Furthermore	• Such as
• Because	• Hence	• While

Kingore, B. (2007). *Reaching All Learners.* Austin, TX: Professional Associates Publishing.

Involve students in evaluating the effectiveness of a summary (Wormeli, 2005). Figure 4.18 is one example of criteria students can use to assess summaries. Analyzing effective and less-effective summaries assists the development of students' understanding of how to create valid summaries.

• **Figure 4.18** •
Criteria for Assessing an Effective Summary

Accuracy	Is the information accurate?
Value	Is this the essence of the content? Could someone gain a valid overview from this summary?
Length	Are all of the key elements included? Is the summary too long or too narrow?
Organization	Is the information in the correct sequence?
Opinion free	Do I omit my opinion and just report the content?
Originality	Are these my own words?

Incorporate summarization frequently to enhance students' memory. Add a summary to familiar graphic organizers to augment the information. When using a Venn diagram, for example, conclude with a summary to add under the listing of similarities and differences.

Kingore, B. (2007). *Reaching All Learners.* Austin, TX: Professional Associates Publishing.

T-TIME

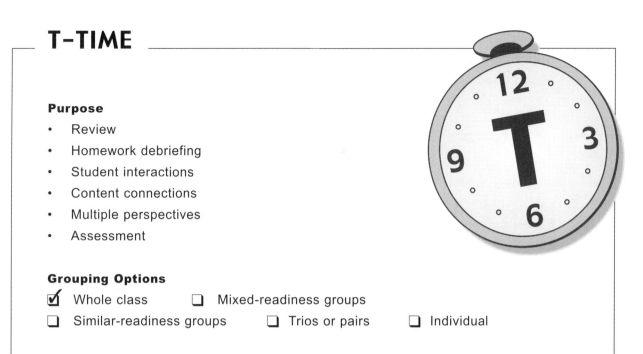

Purpose
- Review
- Homework debriefing
- Student interactions
- Content connections
- Multiple perspectives
- Assessment

Grouping Options
☑ Whole class   ☐ Mixed-readiness groups
☐ Similar-readiness groups   ☐ Trios or pairs   ☐ Individual

What is it?

T-time denotes topic talk or talk to transfer. For five minutes or so, students verbally interact with others to actively share information. They talk about a current topic of study to transfer content and share perspectives.

Applications

Establish a traffic pattern by placing students in two concentric circles, moving in opposite directions. Uses a remote CD control to begin playing music. Students carry a copy of their work with a pencil or pen and walk in their circle pattern. When the music stops, they turn and share their work with a nearby person from the opposite circle until the music begins again. As students move among peers, they hear other perspectives and review the content. The values of this strategy are discussed in Figure 4.19.

Discuss objectives with students before they begin T-time to control potential problems and increase productivity.
- *Talk with someone you have not talked with during T-time this week.*
- *Move quietly and be productive. Use this learning time well.*
- *What is another important goal for T-time today?*

Debrief at the conclusion of T-time to problem-solve and refine the process.
- *Who talked with someone you hadn't talked with yet this week?*

Kingore, B. (2007). *Reaching All Learners.* Austin, TX: Professional Associates Publishing.

- *What did you do well?*
- *What did you notice during T-time?*

• Figure 4.19 •
Values of T-Time

- *Information sharing.* T-time presents a valued opportunity to share information with peers and learn others' perceptions and ideas.
- *Student ownership.* It gives students an authentic responsibility for learning. They must have their work done and be ready to share.
- *Process engagement.* Students reflect upon their own learning.
- *Social interactions.* The process promotes affirmation and affiliation based upon the shared task and information.
- *Flexible grouping.* The process ensures that more students interact with most of the students in the class. Students interact with others outside of their readiness-level group.
- *Less threatening.* T-time is less threatening to quieter, introspective students. Some students are more comfortable sharing content with just one or two others.
- *Student-selected interactions.* Students select whom to talk to but within the focus of working with different people and with the opposite gender.
- *Assessment opportunities.* The teacher carries a small note pad or checklist to write assessment notes and observations as students participate. Teachers can quickly discern if students are less prepared or flawed in their information.

Use T-time for:
- Sharing homework between students at the beginning of the class. *I learned _____. This is what I did to solve _____.*
- Debriefing content between students following a lesson. *I think ____. I wonder ____.*
- Applications after students have been working independently. *This is what I did.*
- Sharing literature as students relate opinions about books. *I read this book, and I think _____.*
- Reading aloud opportunities. Students prepare material to read to peers. The teacher announces *switch* for readers to move to another peer. This variation offers a more active and welcomed change from paired reading.
- Summarizing content. Students review the key concepts from informational text and prepare a summary of the important and interesting information to share.

Kingore, B. (2007). *Reaching All Learners.* Austin, TX: Professional Associates Publishing.

TAPE RECORDING

Purpose
*   Developing background knowledge
*   Enjoying fiction and nonfiction
*   Auditory learning
*   Basic skills
*   Reteaching

Grouping Options
☐ Whole class ☐ Mixed-readiness groups
☐ Similar-readiness groups ☐ Trios or pairs ☑ Individual

What is it?

Tape recordings of class lessons and stories provide a significant auditory learning tool that helps to support ELL students, beginning readers, and students with special needs or fewer skills. Students also listen to tapes of fiction and nonfiction for enjoyment.

Applications

Differentiate instruction through multiple applications using a small tape recorder and inexpensive blank tapes. A tape recording becomes a useful differentiation tool when used with individual earphones. Use file folder peel-off labels to label the content of the tape. Record over the tape when its content is no longer needed.

As an instructional tool for differentiation, tape record:
*   Stories read aloud to the class.
*   A lesson or portions of a lesson that are useful for student practice.
*   Students working in a small group without teacher assistance. The presence of the tape recorder increases their level of concern and task commitment.

Tape recording class stories and other informational content enables ELL students more opportunities to listen to the language. Tapes provide a way for struggling learners to follow along and develop background experience before they read text independently. Furthermore, a tape recording allows all students to select a tape to listen to for enjoyment.

Kingore, B. (2007). *Reaching All Learners.* Austin, TX: Professional Associates Publishing.

Students enjoy the process of making tape recordings and listening to the tapes to hear themselves read or talk. Provide opportunities for students to both listen to tapes and create tape recordings.

Differentiating the Strategy

- A student listens to a tape, following the text, to revisit information and increase comprehension.

- A student quietly reads aloud with a tape recording to enhance fluency and reading skills.

- A student dictates a narrative or expositive piece to listen to and transcribe, thereby practicing writing conventions.

- A student records fiction and nonfiction to create tapes to include in a class listening center.

- A student records research information or the results of a research study to share with others, as in a student-produced research center.

- Each student records a three to five minute reading sample every month on a tape, accumulating these monthly entries. The tape becomes an authentic assessment of reading fluency and complexity level that enables students and parents to appreciate reading growth over time. The tape can be taken home at the end of the year.

Kingore, B. (2007). *Reaching All Learners.* Austin, TX: Professional Associates Publishing.

TEXT CLUBS

Purpose

*   Developing background knowledge
*   Student interaction
*   Analyzing nonfiction
*   Differentiating readability levels
*   Vocabulary

Grouping Options

☐ Whole class   ☑ Mixed-readiness groups

☑ Similar-readiness groups   ☐ Trios or pairs   ☐ Individual

What is it?

The text club strategy involves small, student-centered discussion groups interpreting and responding to nonfiction, topic-related text. The club members form a support system to aid reading comprehension and build background knowledge. One group of three to four students can form a text club, or multiple clubs can form to involve the entire class. The strategy can also provide different levels of complexity in reading materials to respond to the readiness of students.

Applications

> TEACHER: *Did you read the assignment?*
> STUDENT: *I read it but I don't remember what I read.*

This conversation is typical in many classrooms as students seem to turn pages rather than carefully read and comprehend text. These students need strategies that engage them mentally as they read; they would benefit from a support system to aid their comprehension. A text club is a part of this support system. Text clubs supplement instruction by having small groups of students discuss printed information about a topic of study to aid their comprehension and support their development as fluent readers and high-level thinkers. As such, text clubs are a useful component in supporting ELL and struggling readers. Researchers conclude that having students discuss what they read is crucial in developing their ability to construct meaning (Cooper, 2003; Daniels & Bizar, 2005; National Reading Panel, 2000).

Kingore, B. (2007). *Reaching All Learners.* Austin, TX: Professional Associates Publishing.

To expedite active engagement and develop background knowledge, three to four students meet once or twice a week to discuss introductory material as a new topic begins. Brief sessions of ten to fifteen minutes help maintain active participation. The make-up of the group changes when the topic changes so students have ample opportunity to work with different students.

Rather than practice round-robin reading, the students interact to analyze, interpret, and clarify the information. They are encouraged to use the printed material to support their points and read aloud a sentence or section to illustrate a word or idea. At the close of each session, the students decide what needs to be completed before they meet again.

Text clubs can be mixed-readiness groups, but can also be composed of similar-readiness students when the teacher elects to differentiate content with materials at a varied range of readability levels.

Well-prepared students are better able to actively share ideas and respond to the information. To promote preparedness, students complete sticky notes to place in the text as they read. They write questions, ahas, and personal connections that occur to them. Students like sticky-notes as they require a minimum amount of extra time and help students remember ideas. The note also serve as a visual proof of preparation.

When they meet as a club, students share and compare their notes as they discuss the information. If preferred, the teacher can pose one or more questions to focus students' preparation before meeting as a group. The goal is for each member of the text club to participate, pose questions, clarify perceptions, and discuss insights. At the close of the club time, each member develops a simple product that synthesizes the key points in the material, such as a documentation chart, notes, or summarization.

Kingore, B. (2007). *Reaching All Learners.* Austin, TX: Professional Associates Publishing.

THINK ALOUDS

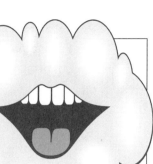

Purpose
- Modeling metacognition
- Comprehension
- High-level thinking
- Informal assessment

Grouping Options

☐ Whole class   ☐ Mixed-readiness groups

☐ Similar-readiness groups   ☐ Trios or pairs   ☑ Individual

What is it?

Think aloud is a metacognitive strategy for monitoring and improving comprehension. Teachers initially model the strategy with students and then encourage students to practice it in small groups. In this approach, teachers verbally share with students the cognitive processes that they go through as they read. By thinking aloud, the teacher makes explicit for students what is implicit for skilled readers so students can develop and apply these strategies themselves.

Applications

The teacher thinks out loud to slow dow   ʼdents get a
clear view of how skilled readers unconsciousl

Research supports the effectiveness
cognitive skills (Baumann, Jones, & Seif
1997). In reading, it is useful for clarifyin
dicting or inferring. In mathematics, it he
labeling procedures, such as breaking
assessment tool—as children bring their
window that increases a teacher's unde

A think aloud is a verbal proce
to articulate out loud what is going on
information. It forces students to think
printed words.

- The st
  need time
  Use think-alou
  avoid the activity
  2001).

Kingore, B. (2007). *Reaching All Lea*

Kingore, B. (2007). *Reaching All Le*

The following partial think-aloud exemplifies how a teacher uses the strategy to model reading and thinking.

> *As I read this paragraph, I am not sure of the subject. It is too ambiguous. After reading more, however, I realize the content is symbolic. The author is using baiting worms as a metaphor for doing something that may seem unpleasant but has an important end result. I like the idea now that I get it. In the next paragraph, the author uses comparison to...*

Students have to be guided in their development of this self-monitoring strategy so the process becomes an internalized part of their regular reading behavior. The process evolves from teacher modeling to collaborative discussions and then to student's independent applications (Figure 4.20).

• Figure 4.20 •
Think Alouds

Steps

1. The teacher reads and thinks out loud as the students listen.
2. The teacher begins a think aloud. The students help out with connections and analyze what to do to address comprehension problems.
3. Students lead a brief think aloud as the teacher and other students facilitate.
4. Students work together in small groups to complete a think aloud about a topic, such as a paragraph.
5. Individual students use a think aloud when they have difficulty extracting meaning from text.

...ategy requires practice. Students who habitually read without comprehending ...o practice before reading and thinking happen simultaneously.

...ds within a specific context or specific comprehension challenge to ...ecoming nothing more than modeling an isolated skill (Oster,

...ners. Austin, TX: Professional Associates Publishing.

- Students should not stop and think aloud after every line of text. Teach them to use the strategy when the meaning is unclear or when they feel that they didn't get anything out of their reading.
- The strategy is used in Chapter 1 of this book to model the thinking processes of teachers as they grapple with differentiating instruction and arrive at decisions.
- To access more information, use *think aloud strategy* as search words for an internet search. Examples of lessons using the strategy and devices for more specifically modeling the process are readily available.

Differentiating the Strategy

- As individual students understand the strategy, they can use it with struggling readers to support their reading and share comprehension insights.
- As an expository writing task, have students write their think aloud process. In addition to an authentic writing activity, the record can be compared to gauge improvement over time or to pinpoint needs for monitoring and assistance.
- Use the strategy with advanced students to model more complex, abstract, or higher-level comprehension processes.

Kingore, B. (2007). *Reaching All Learners.* Austin, TX: Professional Associates Publishing.

TOP TEN

Purpose

- Skill applications
- Content connections
- Informal assessment
- High-level thinking

Grouping Options

- ☐ Whole class
- ☐ Mixed-readiness groups
- ☐ Similar-readiness groups
- ☑ Trios or pairs
- ☑ Individual

What is it?

Students brainstorm and hierarchically rank ten ideas that relate to the topic being studied.

Applications

A favorite feature of the *Late Night with David Letterman* show is his top ten list in which he humorously counts down to the number one or the best item on his list for the topic of the night. Top ten lists can be developed for many education topics and encourage students to consider multiple responses and in-depth thinking.

Content Connections

The teacher states a content specific category that requires students to analyze content and develop a list of ten connections. Then students evaluate their ideas and rank them hierarchically from ten to one, with one being the highest or most significant response. For added novelty and engagement when an individual or group shares a top ten, the rest of the class uses their hands to sound a drum roll before each numbered idea is read. The student who is sharing the top ten signals when the drum roll can begin and end each time an idea is shared. The following examples prompt possibilities for connecting this strategy to content.

- Things to do to learn spelling words
- Best books of all time
- Traits of friendship
- Reasons to go to school
- Errors in place value problems
- Features that define our state
- Presidents who best led our country during troubled times

Kingore, B. (2007). *Reaching All Learners.* Austin, TX: Professional Associates Publishing.

Skill Applications

The top ten strategy effectively initiates skill practice for a wide range of skills. Select a general category that interests students and then post a list of skill applications. Students brainstorm and write ten responses to the category. They draw a star by the idea they think is the best and then select and complete one of the skill applications.

Interesting categories include the following.

- Foods to eat on the weekend
- Things to do after school
- Places you do not want to go
- Questions to which you would say *yes*
- Famous people, from the present or past, who you would like to meet
- Things in pairs
- Favorite things
- Jobs you would like to have
- Questions to which you would say *no*

For ease in preparation, prepare a chart that can be used as the same basic skills are practiced over several days. In other words, the top ten category changes each time but the skill application choices are repeated as appropriate. At the top of the chart, create a template in which a different category is posted each time the strategy is used: *The Top Ten _____.* The remainder of the chart lists the skill applications that are the options for a particular period of time. An example of a top ten chart with skill choices in a fourth grade class is shared as an example in Figure 4.21.

• **Figure 4.21** •
Top Ten with Skill Choices

The Top Ten _____

Skill Choices

- Figure out the total number of syllables in your list.
- Use three of the words in a sentence about your friends.
- Alphabetize your list.
- Write a ten-word sentence about the word on your list that you like most.
- For each word, write an adjective that begins with the initial of your first name.
- Create a symbol for each item. Challenge a classmate to figure out and match your symbols and words.
- Assign values to each letter of the alphabet where A equals one and Z equals twenty-six. Calculate the value of your starred word.

Kingore, B. (2007). *Reaching All Learners.* Austin, TX: Professional Associates Publishing.

TOPIC TALK–
TOPIC TALK AND SWITCH

Topic

Purpose

*   Topic discussion
*   Assessing background knowledge
*   Vocabulary
*   Peer interaction

Grouping Options

☐ Whole class   ☐ Mixed-readiness groups

☐ Similar-readiness groups   ☑ Trios or pairs   ☐ Individual

What is it?

The teacher designates the topic and organizes students to briefly discuss that topic in pairs or trios. At the teacher's signal, students discuss a specific aspect of the topic, pose questions, or produce a specific example. The student pairs toss examples back and forth until they exhaust possibilities or each other.

Applications

The basic process of topic talk is simple so it can be used spontaneously and often. Figure 4.22 on the next page outlines the sequence.

To practice the process, begin with a category of personal interest to students, such as favorite foods or television programs. Then, move to content-related categories, such as verbs, prime numbers, matter, or capital cities.

The teacher can also prompt more complex and conceptual thinking by posing a problem or challenge such as the following.

*   Decide the best approach to this problem.
*   Produce multiple examples of this concept in our community.
*   Determine a key question about _____.
*   Discuss why _____.
*   Discuss what you think is the main idea.
*   Identify and discuss the issues related to _____.

Kingore, B. (2007). *Reaching All Learners.* Austin, TX: Professional Associates Publishing.

• **Figure 4.22** •
Topic Talk

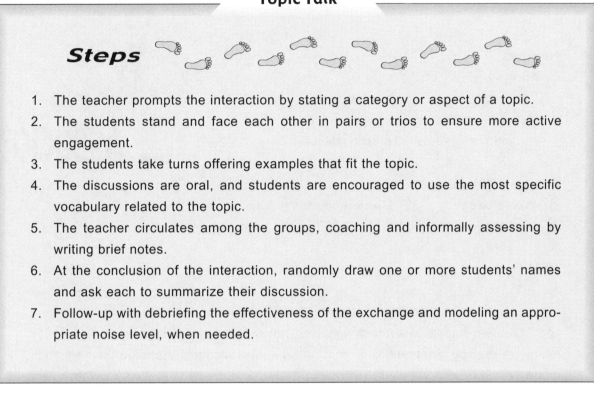

Steps

1. The teacher prompts the interaction by stating a category or aspect of a topic.
2. The students stand and face each other in pairs or trios to ensure more active engagement.
3. The students take turns offering examples that fit the topic.
4. The discussions are oral, and students are encouraged to use the most specific vocabulary related to the topic.
5. The teacher circulates among the groups, coaching and informally assessing by writing brief notes.
6. At the conclusion of the interaction, randomly draw one or more students' names and ask each to summarize their discussion.
7. Follow-up with debriefing the effectiveness of the exchange and modeling an appropriate noise level, when needed.

Topic Talk and Switch

Vary the interaction by asking one member of each pair to begin discussing the topic. When the teacher calls *switch*, the second student in each pair picks up the discussion in mid sentence and continues talking until *switch* is called again. Use a stopwatch or second hand on a watch to keep this interaction moving along at a brisk pace. Student motivation to succeed is increased by the fast pacing and by holding students accountable for learning. As with topic talk, conclude the interaction by randomly drawing one or more students' names and asking each to summarize their discussion.

For novelty, vary topic talk and switch with an ABC response. The students retell a story or significant ideas about a topic by alternating letters of the alphabet in order as they switch back and forth between themselves to respond. For example: ***A** constitution was needed to unite the separate states... **B**enjamin Franklin was one of the statesmen who... **C**alled for...*

Kingore, B. (2007). *Reaching All Learners.* Austin, TX: Professional Associates Publishing.

WORD ASSOCIATIONS

Purpose
- Analysis
- Vocabulary: multiple meaning words
- Multiple contexts
- Art and bodily-kinesthetic applications

Grouping Options
☑ Whole class   ☑ Mixed-readiness groups
☑ Similar-readiness groups   ☑ Trios or pairs   ☑ Individual

What is it?

Word association is a strategy for integrating vocabulary with multiple contexts and multiple meanings. Research supports that vocabulary development is so directly related to reading comprehension that first graders' vocabulary predict their eleventh grade reading comprehension (Marzano, 2004). The larger the reader's vocabulary (either oral or print), the easier it is to understand the text (NRP, 2000).

Applications

It is now known that vocabulary development is more significant than assumed in the past. Students need repeated encounters with words through speaking, reading, writing, and direct instruction in subject-specific vocabulary to develop ownership of previously unknown vocabulary.

Multiple-meaning words directly influence comprehension. Misinterpreting the usage of words impedes understanding and results in errors on standardized tests and learning tasks. Students, particularly ELL and primary children, need experiences with multiple meaning words, but all students benefit from using academic words in meaningful contexts.

Vocabulary should be taught in rich contexts both directly and indirectly (read alouds and sustained silent reading). Words webs and category grids are examples of strategies that directly teach vocabulary. Involving students in games and computer technology applications enhance the acquisition of vocabulary. Additionally, the following strategies, integrate vocabulary in multiple contexts.

QUICK SKETCH

Students sketch images to illustrate a content-specific word. *Sketch what the word means to you. Sketch a picture, symbol, or graphic that represents the term or phrase.*

RESPONSE ROUND

Ask students to respond to prompts inviting them to make personal connections to vocabulary. *This word reminds me of _____. I associate this with _____. Let's see how many different sentences we can make up using the word _____.*

ROLE-PLAY AND VOCABULARY CHARADES

Debra Fraiser's book, *Miss Alaineus: A Vocabulary Disaster* (2000), illustrates an effective combination of role-play and vocabulary when an elementary school has a vocabulary parade in which children act out creative interpretations of a word and the main character dresses up as Miss Alaineus, queen of all miscellaneous things. Combining creative dramatics and productive thinking while activating bodily-kinesthetic responses has a powerful appeal for using vocabulary in multiple contexts.

Role-play and vocabulary charades present a useful means for students to demonstrate their understanding of content-specific words. Involve students in acting out words, as in charades. Encourage them to create role-play scenarios using the word in a meaningful context. Also, read aloud *The Weighty Word Book* (Levitt, Burger, & Gurainick, 2000) to build enthusiasm and generate ideas for students to write scenarios using complex words.

WORD ASSOCIATION CHART

Word association is a game using words in multiple contexts that promotes extensive oral interaction among students. It requires students to use and analyze multiple meaning words in a game environment that is more intellectually risk free. To introduce the game, share a well-known word and then add three words or phrases associating the word in different contexts.
- *Paper, newspaper, paper bag, scrap paper*

Invite students to add to the list. Next, provide three words or phrases and challenge students to figure out the associated word.
- *Honey ___, spelling ___, ___keeper* (the word is: bee)

Kingore, B. (2007). *Reaching All Learners.* Austin, TX: Professional Associates Publishing.

When appropriate, share a chart of word associations for students to decipher. Freely encourage discussion and clarification of contexts among students as they work on the task. Encourage children to seek pictures and examples of any contexts that seem less familiar to them. Figure 4.23 is an example of a word association chart. The answers are: *red, star, tree, house, ball, chair, light, and apple.*

To develop the game using students' vocabulary, reverse the process. Say a word and ask students to quickly write all of the words they can associate with it. Allow only one minute or less for them to write to keep the activity at a fast pace. (Suspending concerns about spelling during this activity increases students' responses.) Briefly encourage students to share results by saying: *Let's share your ideas. Listen carefully and do not repeat a word that someone else says*. As students share, jot down their words.

Use this process as a transition activity or change of pace over several days. After several quick sessions, multiple choices are produced to reorganize into a word association game.

• **Figure 4.23** •

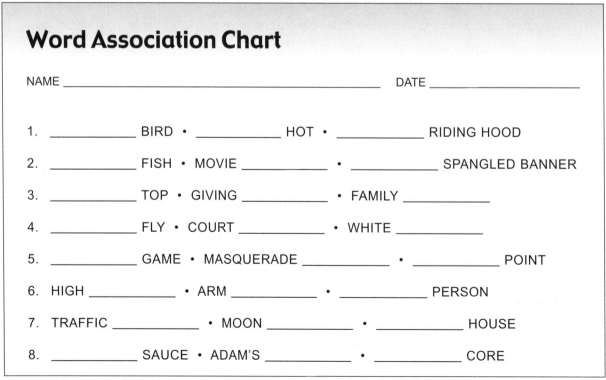

Word Association Chart

NAME _____ DATE _____

1. _____ BIRD • _____ HOT • _____ RIDING HOOD

2. _____ FISH • MOVIE _____ • _____ SPANGLED BANNER

3. _____ TOP • GIVING _____ • FAMILY _____

4. _____ FLY • COURT _____ • WHITE _____

5. _____ GAME • MASQUERADE _____ • _____ POINT

6. HIGH _____ • ARM _____ • _____ PERSON

7. TRAFFIC _____ • MOON _____ • _____ HOUSE

8. _____ SAUCE • ADAM'S _____ • _____ CORE

Kingore, B. (2007). *Reaching All Learners*. Austin, TX: Professional Associates Publishing.

References

Anderson, L. & Krathwohl, D. (Eds.). (2001). *A taxonomy for learning, teaching, and assessing: A revision of Bloom's taxonomy of educational objectives.* New York: Addison-Wesley Longman.

Association for Supervision and Curriculum Development (ASCD). (2006). *Building academic vocabulary: Research-based, comprehensive strategies. Research Report.* Alexandria, VA: Association for Supervision and Curriculum Development.

Baumann, J., Jones, L., & Seifert-Kessell, N. (1993). Using think alouds to enhance children's comprehension monitoring abilities. *The Reading Teacher, 47,* 184-193.

Bradby, M. (1995). *More than anything else.* New York: Orchard Books.

Caine, R., Caine, G., Klimek, K., & McClintic, C. (2004). *12 Brain/mind learning principles in action.* Thousand Oaks, CA: SAGE Publications.

California Association for the Gifted (CAG). (1999). Academic advocacy for the forgotten readers--Gifted and advanced learners. *Communicator, 30*(1), 1, 33-35.

Campbell, L. & Campbell, B. (1999). *Multiple intelligences and student achievement: Success stories from six schools.* Alexandria, VA: Association for Supervision and Curriculum Development.

Cook, N. (2005). Using time-saving technology to facilitate differentiated instruction. *Understanding Our Gifted, 17,*16-19.

Cooper, J. (2003). *Literacy: Helping children construct meaning* (5th ed.). Boston: HoughtonMifflin.

Daniels, H. & Bizar, M. (2005). *Teaching the best practice way: Methods that matter, K-12.* Portland, ME: Stenhouse Publishers.

De Bono, E. (1993). *Teach your child how to think.* New York: Penguin Books.

Eberle, R. (1996). *Scamper.* Waco, TX: Prufrock Press.

Erickson, H. (2007). *Concept-based curriculum and instruction for the thinking classroom.* Thousand Oaks, CA: Corwin Press.

Fleischman, P. (1988). *Joyful noise: Poems for two voices. New York: HarperCollins Publishers.*

Fraiser, D. (2000). *Miss Alaineus: A vocabulary disaster.* San Diego: Harcourt.

Gentry, M. (1999). *Promoting student achievement and exemplary classroom practices through cluster grouping: A research-based alternative to heterogeneous elementary classrooms.* Storrs, CT: The National Research Center on the Gifted and Talented.

Graves, D. (1994). *A fresh look at writing.* Portsmouth, NH: Heinemann.

Hoberman, M. (2001). *You read to me, I'll read to you.* Boston: Little, Brown, and Company.

Kingore, B. (2003). *Just what I need!* Austin, TX: Professional Associates Publishing.

Kingore, B. (2004). *Differentiation: Simplified, realistic, and effective.* Austin, TX: Professional Associates Publishing.

Kingore, B. (2007). *Assessment: Timesaving procedures for busy teachers (*4th ed.). Austin, TX: Professional Associates Publishing.

Kingore, B. (2008). *Teaching without nonsense* (2nd ed.). Austin, TX: Professional Associates Publishing.

Konigsburg, E. (2000). *Silent to the bone.* New York: Aladdin.

Kulik, J. (1992). *Analysis of the research on ability grouping: Historical and contemporary perspectives.* Storrs, CT: The National Research Center on the Gifted and Talented.

Levitt, P., Burger, D., & Guralnick, E. (2000). *The weighty word book.* Lanham, MD: Roberts Rinehart.

Lowry, L. (1989). *Number the stars.* New York: Dell Publishing.

Marzano, R. (2000). *Transforming classroom grading.* Alexandria, VA: Association for Supervision and Curriculum Development.

Marzano, R. (2004). *Building background knowledge for academic achievement: Research on what works in schools.* Alexandria, VA: Association for Supervision and Curriculum Development.

Marzano, R., Pickering, D., & Pollock, J. (2001). *Classroom instruction that works: Research-based strategies for increasing student achievement.* Alexandria, VA: Association for Supervision and Curriculum Development.

National Reading Panel (NRP). (2000). *Teaching children to read: An evidence-based assessment of the scientific research literature on reading and its implications for reading instruction.* Jessup, MD: National Institute for Literacy at ED Pubs.

National Research Council. (1999). *How people learn: Brain, mind, experience and school.* Washington, DC: National Academy Press.

Neeld, E. & Kiefer, K. (1990). *Writing brief* (3rd ed.). Glenview, IL: Scott, Foresman.

Ogle, D. (1986). K-W-L: A teaching model that develops active reading of expository text. *The Reading Teacher, 39,* 564-570.

Oster, L. (2001). Using the think-aloud for reading instruction. *The Reading Teacher, 55,* 64-69.

Paterson, K. (2005). *55 teaching dilemmas: Ten powerful solutions to almost any classroom challenge*. Markham, Ontario, Canada: Pembroke Publication.

Readence, J., Bean, R., & Baldwin, R. (1989). *Content area reading: An integrated approach*. Dubuque, IA: Kendall/Hunt.

Reis, S. (2001). What can we do with talented readers? *Teaching for High Potential, III*(1), 1-2.

Reis, S., Gubbins, E., Briggs, C., Schreiber, F., Richards, S., Jacobs, J., et al. (2004). Reading instruction for talented readers: Case studies documenting few opportunities for continuous progress. *Gifted Child Quarterly, 48,* 315-338.

Rogers, K. (1998). Using current research to make 'good' decisions about grouping. *NASSP Bulletin, 82,* 38-46.

Rosenshine, B. & Meister, C. (1997). Cognitive strategy instruction in reading. In S. Stahl & D. Hayes (Eds.), *Instructional models in reading* (pp. 85-107). Mahwah, NJ: Erlbaum Associates.

Salinger, T. & Fleischman, S. (2005). Teaching students to interact with text. *Educational Leadership, 63,* 90-92.

Schumm, J., Moody. S., & Vaughn, W. (2000). Grouping for reading instruction: Does one size fit all? *Journal of Learning Disabilities, 33,* 477-488.

Shade, R. & Garrett, P. (2002). *Laughing matters! Using humor in classroom activities*. Austin, TX: Professional Associates Publishing.

Shepard, L. (1997). *Measuring achievement: What does it mean to test for robust understanding?* Princeton, NJ: Educational Testing Service.

Sousa, D. (2001). *How the brain learns* (2nd ed.). Thousand Oaks, CA: Corwin Press.

Sousa, D. (2003). *How the gifted brain learns*. Thousand Oaks, CA: Corwin Press.

Sternberg, R., Torff, B., & Grigorenko, E. (1998). Teaching triarchically improves student achievement. *Journal of Educational Psychology, 90,* 374-384.

Stiggins, R. (2001). *Student-involved classroom assessment* (3rd, ed.). Upper Saddle River, NJ: Merrill Prentice Hall.

Stronge, J. (2002). *Qualities of effective teachers*. Alexandria, VA: Association for Supervision and Curriculum Development.

Sylwester, R. (2003). *A biological brain in a cultural classroom* (2nd ed.). Thousand Oaks, CA: Corwin Press.

Tomlinson, C. (2003). *Fulfilling the promise of the differentiated classroom*. Alexandria, VA: Association for Supervision and Curriculum Development.

Vygotsky, L. (1962). *Thought and language.* Cambridge: MIT Press.

Westberg, K., Archambault, F., Dobyns, S., & Salvin, T. (1993). *The classroom practices study: Observational findings.* Storrs, CT: The National Research Center on the Gifted and Talented.

Wiggins, G. & McTighe, J. (2005). *Understanding by design* (2nd ed.). Alexandria, VA: Association for Supervision and Curriculum Development.

Willis, J. (2006). *Research-based strategies to ignite student learning: Insights from a neurologist and classroom teacher.* Alexandria, VA: Association for Supervision and Curriculum Development.

Willis, J. (2007). *Brain-friendly strategies for the inclusion classroom.* Alexandria, VA: Association for Supervision and Curriculum Development.

Wolfe, P. (2001). *Brain matters: Translating research into classroom practice.* Alexandria, VA: Association for Supervision and Curriculum Development.

Wormeli, R. (2005). *Summarization in any subject: 50 techniques to improve student learning.* Alexandria, VA: Association for Supervision and Curriculum Development.

Wormeli, R. (2006). *Fair isn't always equal: Assessing and grading in the differentiated classroom.* Portland, ME: Stenhouse Publishers.

Index